"Reading Gabriela Wiener is a joy. Over the years, her work has made me cry, laugh, hurt, and most importantly, dream. Her essays are daring, intimate, and honest, containing the self-awareness of a poet and the sharp focus of a marksman. I'd follow her anywhere."

DANIEL ALARCÓN
AUTHOR OF *AT NIGHT WE WALK IN CIRCLES*

"No other writer in the Spanish-speaking world is as fiercely independent and thoroughly irreverent as Gabriela Wiener. Constantly testing the limits of genre and gender, Wiener's work ... has bravely unveiled truths some may prefer remain concealed about a range of topics, from the daily life of polymorphous desire to the tiring labor of maternity."

CRISTINA RIVERA GARZA
AUTHOR OF *THE ILIAC CREST*

"One of the sexiest voices of our times."

RODRIGO FRESÁN
AUTHOR OF *KENSINGTON GARDENS*

"Reading her, one has the feeling of an unexpected closeness—a proximity that accelerates one's heart rate. Gabriela Wiener has no scruples when it comes to revealing her sexuality, her suffering, her curiosity, or her morbid obsessions, and this sincerity makes her prose admirable and uncommonly daring."

GUADALUPE NETTEL
AUTHOR OF *THE BODY WHERE I WAS BORN*

"Gabriela Wiener writes about her adventures as a fledgling wild detective; her real and imagined illnesses; her numerological obsessions; her sexuality; and her life as a mother, a wife, and a nostalgic and furious Peruvian. In whispers and in laughter—and ranging from uncertainty to denunciation and from full-frontal exhibitionism to coy flirtatiousness—the author gives herself over to writing. The result is this insolent and amusing book: as journalistic as it is lyrical, by turns sad and delirious, and unforgettable throughout."

ALEJANDRO ZAMBRA
AUTHOR OF *BONSAI*

"[Gabriela Wiener's] self-portrayal changed literary language.... It sees, swallows, metabolizes, grows, speaks, risks, [and] arrives, restless."

MARTA SANZ
AUTHOR OF *FARÁNDULA*

"[Gabriela Wiener's] essays flock like street urchins around unsuspecting readers who, dazed, realize their wallet has been stolen along with everything they thought they knew about themselves. My own wallet, of course, Wiener's long had in her pocket."

PAUL B. PRECIADO
AUTHOR OF *TESTO JUNKIE*

SEXOGRAPHIES

GABRIELA WIENER

SEXOGRAPHIES

Translated from the Spanish by
Jennifer Adcock and Lucy Greaves

RESTLESS BOOKS
BROOKLYN, NEW YORK

First Restless Books paperback edition May 2018

Paperback ISBN: 9781632061591
Library of Congress Control Number: 2017963942

Cover design by Na Kim
Set in Garibaldi by Tetragon, London

Printed in Canada

1 3 5 7 9 10 8 6 4 2

Restless Books, Inc.
232 3rd Street, Suite A111
Brooklyn, NY 11215

www.restlessbooks.org
publisher@restlessbooks.org

CONTENTS

SEXOGRAPHIES

GURU & FAMILY

For La Gatita

IF BADANI WERE AN ELECTRICAL APPLIANCE, he would be one that chops, dices, and shreds his interlocutor at a thousand revolutions per second. When he speaks—or rather when he soliloquizes—he smooths out his mustache with a delicate movement of his thumb and index finger. Erecting an argument or even just assembling a phrase in his presence is impossible. Badani senses your intentions, anticipates your answers, reads your facial expressions, and is wary of your words. It would be foolish to expect any less from him—a man who is a polygamist, tech expert, zealous anti-Catholic, sexual erudite, and devotee of the concept of freedom, which he understands as the liberty to choose one's own shackles. Badani is also addicted to etymology. "Family," he says, "comes from the Latin *famulus*, which means 'slave.'" He has six of them.

Since his life came into the public eye, Ricardo Badani has elicited the hatred of many. He's been denounced as a misogynist and a homophobe, with good reason: his archaic worldview advocates for a return to the time of alpha males and female acolytes. He hasn't varied or nuanced his discourse in the slightest throughout the years. I, on the other hand, have become more radical, especially when it comes to feminism. I've never ceased to disagree with him—not back then, and definitely not now.

But his story continues to fascinate me for many reasons; not the least of them being his defiant choice to live on the fringe of convention, always challenging any sort of restraint.

The man has the beard of a prophet and a perpetual gleam in his eye. He's sitting on a sofa in the lingerie store he runs with his wives in a shopping center in Miraflores, one of the most affluent districts of Lima. He's spent several minutes talking at me about corsets, and I am yet to utter a single word. With a quiet gesture—he touches his throat—one of his wives immediately gets him some Coca-Cola. He's clearly showing off for me. His wives are constantly attending to his every need like abnegated serfs (who nonetheless claim to feel free as a bird). The protector and the slave: that is their ideal definition of a relationship. They become a part of him, and he bears the brunt of society's displeasure. A recycled but revolutionary formula for happiness.

The ideal of equality between men and women is, to him, stupidity masked as erudition. Males and females are united by what they lack, and for Badani, a family is a natural integration of complementary elements. A family is comparable, he says, to a ship. The man is the captain, the women are the officers, and the children are the crew. The crew does not have the right to voice its opinions. The officers can give advice to the captain, but they don't get much of a say when it comes to steering the ship. Captain Badani is solely responsible for the ship, the crew, the cargo, the passengers, and the route.

The second time I interviewed Badani in his shop he said, "The girls liked you. It must be because you did your homework." Before contacting him, I'd read his *Windmill Blades*, a book of short stories and poems featuring him on the front cover dressed as Don Quixote. The guru was aware that what I truly wanted was to visit his house, to spend a day in the Badani family home. To stoke my desire, Badani had delayed giving me an answer for as long as possible.

Years earlier, they had all moved to the outskirts of Lima, where the beastly tentacles of the press could not reach them. Once they'd settled into their new home, he and his wives had vowed to shut out anyone who intended to categorize or diagnose them. That meant no journalists, who in Badani's opinion trade in human misery. But Badani is like a pliant middle-aged father who enjoys making a show out of his leniency—a display there was nothing left but to appear grateful for. And so they laid out the terms for the encounter: no camera, no tape recorder, no notebook.

I phoned the shop on the agreed-to date and spoke to one of his wives, Mara Abovich. She'd been appointed to tell me that Badani had consented to invite me from Tuesday to Thursday. The offer consisted of spending two nights at an unspecified location in Lima with the guru of sex and his six wives. Sensing my hesitation, Mara asked if going to their home was not what I had wanted. It was, but I hadn't imagined the guru would invite me to stay overnight. She told me to bring my toothbrush, and, if possible, some white marshmallows to toast on the fire. The way to the way is the way, says the Tao.

That Tuesday evening, to make sure I'd fit in, I arrived at the shop wearing a skirt. Badani had mentioned that his wives never wear pants. He'd also mentioned that they were fully waxed, but I didn't go that far. When I got there, I glanced at one of the tags on the clothes on the rack: "Badani, instruments of seduction." Mara, the sixth wife, had just arrived. She was carrying several shopping bags that held Italian sausages and other items requested by Badani.

"You'll have to excuse me, Ricardo asked me to do this," she said. Mara then tested my honesty aura with a camera detector bought at RadioShack, where Badani likes to get electronic gadgets.

Mara Irma Abovich resembles her body: she's a compact and vigorous Chilean woman who immediately commands respect. Her speech swings from severity back to jest in an enthralling way. She is perhaps the only one of Badani's wives who doesn't seem to have been fully tamed. From time to time, her insurgent spirit rears its head with a remark whose irony Badani pretends to ignore. Mara tells me she comes from a well-to-do family in Chile. Her story is key to understanding the essence of a Mrs. Badani. She says she was a successful businesswoman in the interior design industry, one of those strong, independent women who, I'd later discover, are somewhat frowned upon in the Badani family. She owned a luxury apartment and traveled the world, but one day she began to feel as though nothing made sense. Until she saw Badani giving a conference about Tantra.

"Wasn't your boyfriend worried when you said you were going to spend the night at Badani's house?" she asks me, out of the blue.

"To be honest, he wasn't thrilled."

"With good reason," she says to my surprise.

The first time she went to see the Badanis, Mara Abovich remembers thinking they were a bunch of outlandish characters. Fairly interesting ones, but lunatics nonetheless.

"But as you can see, I became the sixth wife. This lifestyle is irresistible. Maybe you'll become number seven."

I feel a comical shiver run down my spine.

Saraswati, the Goddess of Wisdom, rules Mara's life. According to her religion, her day off is Saturday. Each of Badani's wives has one day off a week, a day when she can do whatever she wants, is exempt from household chores, and gets to sleep with the husband in his king-size bed. Today's day off is Gaby's—my namesake.

Genealogies: Badani's real name is Ricardo Ruiloba. His surname was changed, he tells me, in the midst of a family dispute. His father was Luis María Ruiloba, a lawyer who separated from Teresa Badani when the future guru of sex was only three years old. Ruiloba is an Asturian surname that means "lord of the wolves." It's also the title of the unpublished novel that Badani dedicated to his father, in which he expounds upon his theory of clans as the basis of an ideal society.

Any mention of his family makes him as defensive as an abandoned little boy. Badani gets emotional when he reminisces on Luis María Ruiloba. His father's absence seems to have, surprisingly, improved him rather than traumatized him. But when I mention his brother Bernardo, who is three years his senior, his face grows somber. He says they'd never been particularly close, but he never expected his brother to turn his back on him the way he did when Badani and his wives returned to Peru. Overinflated sibling disputes are so common that it's impossible to know whether Badani is joking when he says his brother works as a glorified potato chip vendor. Many moons have passed since they rode their bikes through the sun-bathed vines at the Venturos's hacienda, where Grandfather Badani, who was like a father to the Ruiloba brothers, used to live. Theirs was a typical middle-class Catholic family. But Badani is done discussing the subject now.

Someone told me that the writer and traveler Rafo León had gone to school with the guru, and I contacted him to ask about those days when they had shared a classroom in the Champagnat de Miraflores school. He remembered the Ruiloba Badanis perfectly: "Two identical brothers, pale, sickly-looking, very pedantic, and total nerds." Throughout their school years, the brothers won every academic prize there was. Ricardo Badani was awarded diplomas in science, literature, and good behavior, as well as eleven gold medals for each of the eleven years of his school career. According to León, the boys' mother and aunt were good friends with the Marist priests. They were allowed to interrupt class in the middle of the morning just to bring the boys a tray with papaya juice and buns.

To León they were cold, withdrawn geniuses. He thought they were bound to become priests, or, in the best of cases, homosexuals. A few years ago, he was surprised to learn that the younger brother had six wives and was considered an expert on sexuality. León can't help but think of Badani's polygamy as some kind of settling of scores. Another classmate, Manuel San Román, had also thought the perfectly behaved teenager was doomed to the cassock. He has his own theory about the guru:

"Living with one woman is difficult enough. Can you imagine living with six? The guy is a genius."

Badani warns me that I've been allowed into his house because I'm being given the benefit of the doubt. He tells me he'll reserve judgment on me until my story is published. The door to the Badani home opens, and I'm greeted by the slipper-clad guru and his yappy dogs: the ultra-loyal Taffy, Lucky, and Cindy, who have perfectly substituted children for many years. Once inside the house I see, for the first time, all six wives together.

In order of their arrival in his life: 1. Elsa, 2. Gaby, 3. Lola, 4. Mercedes, 5. Beatriz, 6. Mara. One in six, as Badani calls them. I eye them: they're all over thirty and wear bright colors, but each has their own style. I feel like they're taking my invasion very well. If they've learned anything during their years of cohabitation, it's sharing with other women.

One of the questions that Badani and his wives will repeat several times during my visit is whether their house is the way I'd pictured it. To tell the truth, it isn't. Sometimes I'd imagined it as a small palace á la the Taj Mahal, other times as a shack for mystics. But it's neither. In the front garden, an idyllic swing seat sways in the wind. Badani guides me to his favorite spot, a cozy bar where he keeps an impressive wine reserve. To liven up the welcome tour, Badani fixes me a cocktail, a skill he acquired back when he hosted a television show. He's a mad scientist behind the bar. He invents new drinks and obsessively records how many minutes each one of the liquors takes to enter the bloodstream when mixed in a beverage of his own invention, named "Amnesia" in honor of its effects.

Badani says he bought the house at a bargain with part of the money from the sale of his ranch near Santiago de Chile, although he also admits it has cost a fortune to renovate. He says this with the same pride with which he talks about his sexual prowess or his IQ. The living room is austerely rustic—no Persian rugs, veils, alabaster, or golden statues in sight. There is a computer room next door and a library upstairs, which holds a magnificent selection of erotic literature, an illustrated edition of the *Kama Sutra*, and a sizable collection of erotic films, including classics such as *Story of O*. A veritable feast for lovers of eroticism that, at Badani's suggestion, I'm planning to enjoy before going to bed. The bedrooms surround the library. To the right of the stairs are the two rooms shared by the wives, with three single beds in each. The décor might be called minimalist, if you're feeling generous—an enclosed convent with no trace of their personalities, no feminine details, and no ornaments attributable to any one of them, except for the odd soft animal on a pillow. To the left of the staircase is the husband's room, with an enormous bed, a built-in wardrobe, and a "do not disturb" sign on the door. Tonight, I'm told, I'll be sharing the room with Mara and Beatriz. I'll get Gaby's bed, as it's my namesake's turn to sleep with Badani.

I'm called downstairs to help decide on the dinner menu. We have two options: "Badani soup" (noodles, chorizo, olives, ham, chicken, cheese, and beef), or sausages roasted in the fireplace. Beatriz, ignoring both options, asks to be indulged with a pizza, and the matter is settled. This is how decisions are made in this household. While five of them work in the kitchen, Badani shows me to the rustic sofa in the living room. La Gatita, as he calls Mercedes, will belly dance for me. I'm given a front-row seat. La Gatita, dressed in a golden, gem-embroidered outfit and pearled in sweat, shimmies her waist and her breasts at my eye level like a woman possessed, while Badani puts a damper on things by breaking down, like a stuffy academic, each phase of the dance: the gaze, the offering, the delivery. At the end of the dance, Badani slides his hand down La Gatita's panties and removes it, moist and shiny, with a gynecological flourish.

"If a woman isn't wet after this dance," he explains to me, "then she has not danced it properly. Mercedes has danced it to perfection."

Tomorrow La Gatita will give me a belly dance lesson. But for now, it's time to eat pizza. We discuss female ejaculation over dinner. They claim they can help me ejaculate with an infallible technique. They tell me they have a gynecologist's speculum and that I'm free to use it if I want to observe the exact moment of my orgasm. Everything is natural, harmonious. Everything is a discovery. Everything is so perfectly, archetypally "Badanian" that I ask if this is a hidden camera stunt.

Badani boasts of his intelligence. He even provides stats about his IQ. He says when he was very young he put an ad in the paper: "Brain for hire—young, bilingual man in top form." That's how he got his first job as an administrative services assistant at a petrol station. Three months in, he had his boss's job. He tells me he was liberated by the realization that there was only one reason he pursued a financially stable career: he wanted to have a family.

He did very well for himself in the tech industry. He launched a successful career in IT, and his software start-up, miniCOMP, was one of the first in Peru. In the early 1990s, Badani traveled to Chile in search of new business opportunities. He says he was an IT adviser for companies such as Apple. I suspect that the family never discusses the subject of finances. It's up to the husband to figure out how to earn money, and the wives don't meddle. Nowadays, Badani offers software services from his independent company Gurú&Familia. He and his wives set up the erotic clothing store in 2001. The whole family is responsible for the clothing designs, the production, and the sales. With the store and some conferences—such as the one Badani gave recently at the Society of Jewish Women—this heptagonal family earns a good living. To those who think Badani must be a millionaire in order to sustain six wives, he responds: "modern parasites that call themselves independent women are much more expensive." I let that one slide.

Badani says he was born in a clan of "Cathocrazies." He explains that he was too intelligent to keep on lighting candles for the biggest multinational in the world, which begs for alms from the poor while drinking from cups of gold. "Only when the Cardinal of Lima works as a carpenter in the Comas district will I have any faith in him." He is no longer the Badani who years ago promoted youth Masses with electric guitar performances in the Episcopal Commission. One of his wives shows me a Catholic rock LP that Badani recorded back then. His relationship with the Catholic Church ended the way love affairs tend to: a priest wanted him to believe a blatant lie, and that was the end of it.

Badani was in search of something deeper. He studied the Bible with Mormons, prophesied with Jehovah's Witnesses, preached with Evangelists, tried esotericism, learned to read the tarot, and ended up yielding to the seductions of the Tao and yoga. He was studying the latter when a friend told him that a yogic guru was visiting from India. Badani remembers being initially unimpressed by the disheveled man and his elementary English. Then the guru started speaking about nuclear physics. He told Badani he was inhabited by entire solar systems, and invited him to praise divinity with his infinite body and mind. They crossed paths again a year later in the same street in downtown Lima, and Badani was initiated. What he never could have suspected is that his teacher would elect him as his successor. Badani's wives call him "gurunyi," which means "my guru." He says he has one of the highest ranks in a five-thousand-year-old religion. Tantra adores a binary God's masculine (Shiva) and feminine (Shakti) energies. But the Badanis' Tantrism has nothing to do with the widely publicized, New Age concept of Tantra as a purely sexual technique. It goes beyond that: it seeks the realization of the human being through acceptance of sexuality as an essential part of life. Men can have up to six wives, one for each working day of the week. It is said that Shiva has just one incarnation: the erect penis. On the other hand, Shakti has six facets. Monday corresponds to Lord Shiva and the masculine—that is, Badani—is worshipped. On Tuesdays Gaby is adored, on Wednesdays Elsa, on Thursdays Beatriz, on Fridays Mercedes, on Saturdays Mara, and on Sundays Lola. Badani is living the dream. He would rather be a mad Don Quixote, he tells me, than die of indigestion in bed, Sancho Panza–style.

It's hard to imagine that this man, who now makes love to six women, was once a shy boy who had his first girlfriend at the age of nineteen. Badani lost his virginity at a brothel. He'd had several girlfriends before getting married, but none of them were memorable. He was already giving talks on the teachings of Tantra when he met Elsa Linares, a secretary and an excellent cook from the region of Loreto in the northeast of Peru. They fell in love, but before sealing their commitment, Badani broke the news:

"My guru revealed to me that I'll marry several women."

He asked her to think it over, but Elsa Linares didn't need to. He says it was she who, years later, suggested he think about marrying Gabriela Amor Zevallos (not only is she my namesake but her second name is *amor*), who'd come to the Badanis' house to take a computing course. One day, the couple were lying in bed when Elsa asked the surprised Badani if he thought Gabriela Amor would make a suitable second wife. Badani then met Lola, short for Aurora Revollé, at a friend's restaurant. Not long after, he met Mercedes Morales at one of his talks. Badani then moved to Chile with his quartet of wives. Beatriz González would join them after hearing him talk on the radio about the Big Bang. The last wife, Mara Abovich, was drawn in by curiosity. And so they celebrated the Ceremony of Eternal Union and vowed to share their lives without jealousy. ("Seven without jealousy is heaven," reads the tagline on their website.)

For Badani, a polygynous family consisting of one man and several women is stronger and more stable than a monogamous one. He recently celebrated his eleventh anniversary with his sixth wife, and is about to celebrate his twenty-third with the first. Badani is living proof that his experiment works.

Some advantages of being a Badani: if a wife doesn't want to sleep with her husband, it doesn't matter because there's always another woman. No more sexual blackmail. When there are any disagreements, there is such a thing as a woman who helps the husband understand the other woman, which doesn't tend to happen in a monogamous relationship. And if the husband dies, they all have a way of earning a living together. Another advantage of polygyny: cleaning the house is much faster.

The Badani women made public their firm commitment to accepting, in the midst of the twenty-first century, the shackles of love, making them a kick in the gut to any disciple of Simone de

Beauvoir. Many consider them the flock of a depraved shepherd, but upon meeting them are surprised to find them friendly and intelligent. These are women who know what they want, and whether it was only a charade staged for me (no family can be that perfect), I didn't get the slightest impression that anything they did was against their free will. For Badani's wives, it was a matter of choice. They had the opportunity to be emancipated women, as others are, but instead they chose this peculiar way of being free.

The next day, all six wives got up at five in the morning. I wonder if they maintain that same early-bird enthusiasm every single day. Beatriz and I do the dishes from last night's pizza. She says the goddess of prosperity and devotion rules her life. She's slim and fragile-looking. Because I know she likes reading erotic novels, I tell her that last night I made a dent in *Viaje al deseo* (*Journey to Desire*) and she tells me about the novel she's writing. Breakfast is ready. Orange juice, melon, blackberry jam, coffee, and leftover pizza. Badani spoils me with a cheese and salami wrap he prepared just for me. Then it's time for the "Gayatri," a mantra sung by the whole family. After breakfast, they invite me to the *mandir*, their temple. The women all put veils on their heads and give me one, too. Badani asks me to choose a direction to face and I choose north, which, he says, means I have peace in my heart. I close my eyes. The six wives surround me in what they call a "circle of *biyas*." The mantras the women sing are heavenly, their melodious tones and Badani's deep voice create a harmony that moves me to the point of goose bumps.

When the hour of mystical rapture is over, I'm off to get fit with Gaby Amor. The gym—a converted garage space—is fully decked out. Badani pokes fun at my ineptitude when it comes to step aerobics. Gaby Amor is probably one of the most practical among the women in the household: she's an IT systems expert who carries around Taffy, a black, hairy, flealess baby. She's in charge of managing the household bills and accompanies Badani on his errands and trips. They say she is the goddess mother of warriors, the one who protects their children. It's weird: I swear Gaby Amor has the face of a Hindu goddess. I go upstairs covered in sweat, and before taking a shower poke my head into the guru's bedroom. He's apparently also an expert in acupuncture: Lola is lying on the bed with several needles stuck in her back and feet. Lola, architect by trade, is perhaps the least effusive and most serious of the six wives. Her goddess is the protective mother. In the shower, I remember the inconspicuous security cameras Badani had pointed out earlier, and I can't help but wonder whether there aren't more around the house. I try out my most coquettish smile, just in case.

Badani is a splendid host—attentive to the point of being overwhelming. He indulges me with chocolates and tells me I can do whatever I want, giving me the impression that, in this regime of agreed-upon slavery, today is my day off. He positively spoils me, which is slightly disturbing for someone who comes from a matriarchal family like myself. I feel disgustingly comfortable in a place where us women are paid with flattery.

Mercedes is the pretty one, the family's artist, the one who gives massages and haircuts, the goddess of mercy. She says her greatest blessing is her devotion to her husband. She enjoys role play, writing, and reading in English and French. You can see from a mile off that she's the guru's pet, but just in case his devotion wasn't evident enough, he built her a mirrored dance room with parquet flooring—the place where I agreed to meet Mercedes for my lesson. We tie scarves around our hips and knot our T-shirts under our breasts, leaving our stomachs uncovered. I am the wife of Ali Baba. Mercedes teaches me to look at myself in the mirror, to confront my sensuality, to seduce with my gaze, to reveal my belly as I swing my hips to the rhythm of "The Girls of Alexandria." Badani enters and, without asking, takes a picture of me in the middle of a hip-swinging trance. La Gatita has graciously pronounced me a natural. I lap it all up.

By the end of the night, I want to be like these women. I want to be lavished with heart-shaped sweets and chocolate roses. I want my work to be a hobby. I want to live with all of my best friends and play amorous games together. I want to embroider panties and bras. I want to cook for my man. I want to wear Arabian fantasy clothes. I want to love the present. I want a god.

A cautionary tale: The Badanis lived on a remote farm in Los Maquis, a town two hours south of Santiago. They grew legumes and kept sheep. Gaby Amor tells me the police traveled all the way to Los Maquis to wage war on them, to remind them that religious persecution still exists, in its most lumpen version. She says around twenty armed policemen from the Sexual Offenses Unit broke into the farm. There were also television cameras. At the same time, the police in Santiago raided the house of another member of their same religion. They were all arrested and taken to the Santiago Investigative Police cells, where they had to go on a hunger strike to persuade the consul of Peru to come to their aid. They were accused of being a sadomasochist sect that kept women captive against their will. Gaby says they were beaten up, some of them were tortured, and the women were forced to strip naked. The authorities eventually released them because they found no condemning evidence (that is, because there had been no crime in the first place). The Badanis were deported from Chile on the basis of the same charges that they had already been absolved of. Their appeal is still ongoing with the OAS, Gaby Amor tells me, her Hindu goddess eyes aflame.

Tabloid news from back when Fujimori was Peru's president: Ricardo Badani, a Peruvian man with a harem of six wives, the so-called guru of sex, has been imprisoned and faces charges of sadomasochism and depravity. It sold papers. As soon as they stepped off the plane in Lima they were hounded by the press. They became journalistic carrion. They hadn't asked for fame; it had been imposed on them. But by then there was nothing they could do but take advantage of it. The whole family took part in the production of a TV show. Sitting in the library's most comfortable sofa, I watch a VHS anthology of the show's most stellar scenes. I still find it incredible that they were broadcast on our prudish national television. Never had sex been treated with such clinical audacity.

Snapshots from the annals of television:

Scene 1, Badani's birthday party: The wives' birthday gift is a stripper who emerges from an immense cake and performs a strip-tease on live broadcast. Behind them, their distinguished guests, very elegantly dressed, give a slow, slightly confused applause.

Scene 2: Natalia Torres Vilar, an eminent theater actor, shares her experiences of anal sex.

Scene 3: In an homage to cunnilingus, Badani exhibits an uncensored home video where a couple wearing masks practice oral sex. Everything is in full view, a mouth-to-genitals close-up. Badani uses a laser pointer and technical language to describe the sensitive parts of a woman's genitalia.

The show was broadcast daily at midnight. It was canceled within a month.

In the early evening, everyone gathers in the living room to choose where to hang the joke Olympic gold medal that the wives gave Badani on their last collective anniversary. It's inscribed "to the best husband in the world." The other side reads: "for outstanding stamina."

Each wife sleeps with Badani on their respective day off, but they're well aware that love knows no calendar constraints. On any given night, Badani might end up with one wife or with all six. A poem written by Badani evokes the plenitude of their love: "Their breasts surround me / their erect breasts / of tantalizing curvature / hard nipples / which my lips part / they place in my hands / heart and blood / pulsating in all six. / Their vulvas surround me / their vulvas bathed / in fragrant aroma." Badani might be in bed making love to two of them when a third one comes in with cookies and something to drink for the exhausted lovers. They are seven musketeers: all for one and one for all.

Someone once proposed in some magazine that Badani be named minister of health for his impeccable family planning. All hail his birth control techniques! Badani admits he was warned by his guru not to have children if he wanted to preach his creed. Badani saved himself the risk of spending money on custody trials or of losing his children to the Child Protection Services, as had happened to a Mormon recently in the United States. La

Gatita tells me she and the rest of the women take pride in their decision not to have children. The essence of their religion is to imitate the divine union, and their creed defines fruitfulness not in terms of how many children are brought into the world and indoctrinated, but in terms of its parishioners' devotion to the union between man and woman. In other words, fucking like crazy is their way of worshipping God. Amen.

The "sex guru" moniker was coined by the press. Badani gladly donned the term: "I am the one who leads you from *gu* [darkness] to *ru* [light], the one who brings you out of ignorance." He says Tantra is a four-story building and the ground floor is our body. In order to reach the other spheres, we must start by learning to use our sexuality. That's why Badani is so serious about his mission to teach us mortals how to explore the possibilities of our bodies. His television program, *Las noches de Badani*, was part of this charitable agenda. One of his dreams is to one day set up a clinic and an academy of sex. Now I know that getting me to use a speculum, teaching me how to striptease, and discussing female ejaculation at the dinner table weren't for show. He was serious.

I realized just how serious he was when he asked me to accompany him to the garden. Night was falling. It was my last night at the Badani home. The wind was pushing the white swing seat, where the wives liked to sit with their colorful skirts on cool summer nights. I think that Badani, who took to heart the most idiotic feminine stereotypes, hoped I would also enjoy swinging under the stars of Chosica. And he was not mistaken. We sat in the swing seat while two of his dogs sniffed and peed on the flowerbeds.

Now that he had a captive audience, he began his long-winded speech. The polygynist doctor was trying to convince me to undergo a session of high-voltage sexual therapy, courtesy of him and his six loyal nurses.

By that point, we'd revealed more to each other than we probably should have. My double-edged method for gaining interviewees' confidence has always been to make confessions of my own. As I drip-fed details of my love life, my sexual experiences, my promiscuous past, my repressed desires, and my frustrations, the Badanis increasingly forgot that they were in the presence of a journalist. They'd learned that I was intrigued by group sex, but instead of inviting me to participate in a family orgy, they offered me something far better: to discover, through their particular application of Tantra, "unknown corners of my body" and my "'G,' 'H,' and 'I' spots." I'd begun to consider theirs a nearly conventional family, but the invitation reminded me that they were—what? A gang of pervs? Good Samaritans from an orgasm sect? Would they be capable of doing something against my will? Or worse, did I not have any willpower left at all?

I expressed my hesitations as best I could. He insisted. I was several miles away from Lima; nobody, not even Jaime, my partner, knew the address of this house. I was trapped with someone who had once been accused of keeping sexual slaves and of leading a "sect of sadomasochists." I refused once more. A certain sense of ethics prevented me from doing it—I had a boyfriend, I was there to write an article. What's more, and this I didn't say to him, he was scaring me. I was much younger than them. I was alone. I liked Badani but, unlike his wives, I didn't find him sexually attractive. The man seemed unhinged, was looking at me with his little pleading eyes and cornering me with words on the swing seat. And yet a part of me felt that I should not pass up such a unique sex ed lesson. What part of my identity was hesitating to give in—the journalist or the woman? I was sure his wives would take care of me. Some of them were already venerable menopausal women.

The polygynist knew I trusted his wives, so he called on the youngest, Mercedes. Badani asked her to explain the procedure and help put my fears at ease. La Gatita was tall and dark, with black curls that tumbled down her slender, lightly slouched back. She had very long legs, big breasts, and her hips and waist were chiseled by her rigorous belly dance workouts. The previous night she'd showered with me to teach me "how to bathe my man," a technique that basically consisted of hugging his balls with my breasts. She dressed like the others, with wide flower-print skirts and shirts in primary and electric colors.

Badani's well-chosen bait told me that there was no need to worry, that having sex with the guru was not a part of the process. All I'd have to do was undress and lie on the bed as she and the other wives followed their husband's instructions, bringing me to experience a fountain of orgasms that would make me see the phallus of Lord Shiva himself. As La Gatita tried to sell me on the idea of a sexual El Dorado, all sorts of forces were competing inside me. I wondered whether I should continue or if it would be better to do what most would do, and run for the hills.

I decided to go upstairs and investigate. All the wives were already waiting for me in one of the shared rooms, where the beds had been placed all in a row. I discovered that the Badanis had a monumental collection of top-of-the-range vibrators. Some weren't even vibrators, but large contraptions whose seismic vibrations were designed to massage people with severe back problems. I undressed and lay down on one of the beds so that Mara and La Gatita could caress and stimulate me with all their instruments. Badani gave instructions, and from time to time would touch me in the same surgical style of his explicit sexology show. When my clitoris felt tired and fed up with the vibrations, they persuaded me to carry on. I would continue and another orgasm would catch me by surprise. We spent one long hour like that. It was intense, educational, and although it didn't change my understanding of my sexuality, in some way it did expand my horizons.[1]

---

1 Weeks later, I wrote and published the piece without a single mention of what I've just described. When I finally left that house, I didn't have the slightest intention of telling anyone what had happened, not even Jaime. At first, I felt vaguely dirty and confused, as if I'd committed an infidelity. But the primary reason why I didn't describe this was my concern for the safety of the Badanis themselves. When asked how I handle other people's stories, I can only provide one answer: I'm rarely more concerned with literature or journalism than with people's lives. Back then, Badani and his wives still feared reprisals for their way of life. They are undoubtedly a group of people with very specific beliefs, but as far as we know, they have never harmed anyone. They lead a potent sexual life, try to convert people, and, as was revealed to me later in conversations over email, practice BDSM—but neither I nor the state should have any right to legislate in their bed or denounce their sexuality. Although our ideas about gender politics are worlds apart, I always felt empathy for them. Their religious and sexual rights were violated and have not been restored. They are not allowed to return to Chile and their names are kept on file by Interpol. I decided not to put them in danger. Why am I revealing this now? Because I am no longer afraid and I hope that neither are they, even if they continue to fight for their rights. La Gatita died in January 2014 from cancer. In the last days of her illness, she recorded a video where she calls on the International Court of Human Rights to pass a favorable sentence on the case of the violations they suffered in Chile. "What people find most scary about us is the combination of a non-Christian religion and an open and unapologetic sexuality," says La Gatita on the video. Incredible as it may seem, their expulsion from Chile happened twenty years ago and those responsible have not yet been brought to justice.

After I had showered, we sat around the fireplace for dinner. There were marshmallows, the guru played medieval hymns on a Japanese synthesizer and strummed criollo waltzes on his guitar. We ate sausages grilled on the fire and sang a waltz that seemed like a tongue twister. That night I would sleep in La Gatita's and Lola's room, and tomorrow I'd leave first thing in the morning.

The sixth wife, Mara, told Badani she'd joked about me becoming his seventh wife.

Badani said, "Nonsense. Tell your boyfriend that if I'd known he existed, I'd never have invited you. Or at least I would've asked his permission first."[2]

---

2 When Badani read my story of the days I'd spent at his house, he liked it so much that he invited Jaime (who was not yet my husband) and me for lunch. After serving us a veal steak so spicy it made us break into sweats, he offered Jaime his six wives and the family's "sex slave," a very young girl who had dressed as an odalisque for the occasion. They confessed they'd had her leave the house on the days of my visit to avoid going into too much detail about their more alternative pastimes. "My wives are always wet," Ricardo boasted again. "Want to see?" He encouraged Jaime to introduce his fingers into the girl's vagina. The Badanis then invited us to participate in a session like the one I had undergone, but this time as a couple, with the know-how of the sexologist and his wives, who would teach us new tricks and raise the sexual bar. At the end of the day, after we had all prayed together, Badani told Jaime that he (Badani) would die very soon, that he feared for his wives' future. And then he let it drop: he was looking for a successor. He had seen potential in Jaime. We should think it over and seriously consider following his example. I never saw Badani again. Years later, he sent me an email telling me he was studying journalism, and said I'd inspired him. Turns out he didn't convert me, but I converted him. Or perhaps he did convert me. After all, I now have a husband and also a wife. And we're all happy.

IN THE PRISON OF YOUR SKIN

I'M IN LURIGANCHO PRISON, home to some of the most dangerous murderers, thieves, drug dealers, and rapists in Peru, and I'm all by myself. The previous day I'd spurned police protection despite warnings against walking around the prison alone. I'd already visited several times in the company of the warden—and by now most prisoners knew I was a reporter and that I was giving away money and cigarettes in exchange for a picture of their tattoos. Those visits had allowed the photographer to capture some striking images of inked skin, but I'd tired of getting such a peppy, tailored tour of the place, with lunch thrown in for good measure. I decided to come to the prison like any woman wanting to meet with an inmate would.

Following the instructions to a T, I wore a long skirt, sandals, carried ID, and a hat for camouflage. I brought a loaf of bread and a roll of toilet paper to appear more convincing. I was supposed to meet Calambrito, a young prisoner who'd promised to guide me through this inferno, but I didn't have the slightest idea how to find him without blowing my cover.

Luckily, I ended up queuing beside a girl who, like me, was on her way to block twenty. By imitating her, I was able to navigate all the security checkpoints and get through unnoticed. I wondered if this girl's name was inscribed in bleeding letters surrounding a thorny heart on the chest of some murderer, but decided not to pry. To all these queueing women, the man they're visiting inside is innocent. I remember spotting an enormous white and blue dolphin swimming on the dark arm of a woman who stood amidst that sea of wives, lovers, daughters, prostitutes, friends, aunts, and cousins. I seized the opportunity to compliment her on her tattoo, hoping for some comment on the dolphin's meaning, but she ignored me.

I'd later learn that animal tattoos nearly always reference a criminal's alias. Dolphin was, probably, this woman's husband, accompanying her on her skin. The lady behind me, whose son had been in prison for 125 days, glared at me and informed me that "tattoos are for criminals." I was given the number 864—my turn in line—and as the guard was writing it in permanent marker on my forearm, my friend found her husband and said goodbye to me, abandoning me at the door to block twenty.

It was as if all of Peru's criminals had moved into the most frightening neighborhood of Lima. And they all seemed to be roaming pretty freely. Until five in the afternoon, they are all allowed to move about unrestrained: they work, kill, get high, get tattoos, father children, buy electrical appliances, operate in gangs, and monitor robberies from their blocks using cell phones. I nudged a dozing policeman and asked him after Calambrito. "He's in solitary." The uniformed man asked me to wait for another officer to see if he could get him out of "the Pit," the cells where prisoners ended up if they were found in the yard after 5 p.m., usually because they had been shut out of the blocks due to fights or robbery. They could be confined in the Pit for up to fifty days.

The maximum authority of the prison is the warden, Colonel Valdivia. The Colonel is as serious and formal as Vargas Llosa's character Pantaleón Valdivia, who is in charge of creating a regiment of female visitors to appease the passions of the soldiers in the Peruvian jungle. And the Colonel's job is at least as novelesque as his literary counterpart's: he has to control 7,200 prisoners living in a prison built for a fifth of its current population.

I put my glasses on to better read the hieroglyphics of their scars. I riffle through skin after skin, letting the ugliness of their unwashed bodies speak to me.

Researchers who have studied prison tattoos say that they're an identity card of sorts—a language through which the lacerated bodies communicate their lacerated lives. They are marks of marginality, violence, and resistance.

At the start of the twentieth century, the fathers of criminal anthropology hypothesized that tattoos were symbols of psychic primitivism, and they traveled around the world visiting countless prisons to diagnose the degeneration of inmates' souls. They'd hoped to sort criminal pathologies into orderly categories, but the impulse to categorize is often futile. For example, take Cirilo— thrice imprisoned for murder and robbery and living proof that it is not easy to understand evil. On the back of his arm, Cirilo has a faded tattoo of a woman stabbed with a dagger. He says it represents his perplexingly terrible luck with women. This affliction really shouldn't come as a surprise to him—he killed his brother-in-law by stabbing him in the leg.

The life of criminals is as clichéd as their stick-and-poke tattoos: a rose underlined with the name of their deceased mother, saints and sorrowful Christs, voluptuous women, and palm trees with sunsets in the background. Sarita Colonia, the Peruvian patron saint of thieves and rapists, covers many a horrible scar. Ferocious cobras and birds of prey signify strength, skulls indicate a murderous intent, and a snake wrapped around a sword announces the inmate's desire to exact vengeance on the cop that landed them in jail.

They all miss someone, they're all prisoners of someone's love, they all reminisce on their happy days, and recall their childhood idylls. Then their film darkens and they see themselves turning to alcohol, drugs, and crime. The marks on their skin are meant to transport them to better times, to a mother with open arms or a girlfriend waiting for them outside. If Plato had set foot in Lurigancho, he'd take back that famous phrase: "the body is the prison of the soul." The prisoners' tattooed bodies are vehicles for escape, but for now, they are alone. And this devastating loneliness is to blame for everything. Loneliness and that two-faced bitch who stopped coming around. Tattoos are their only loyal companions. They are as everlasting as God.

So this is the Pit, a damp, dead-end alley made up of rows of cells slammed shut with heavy locks. In the half-light, all I can see are the hands of the immured men fluttering between the bars. Outside, prisoners hold their loved ones and blast music, but the festive spirit stops short at the entrance to this dismal block of cells. "Calambrito!" I call out. "Here," they all reply in unison. They're all Calambrito. "Who's looking for him?" replies a voice. Then I yell my own name. Someone tells me to go and find a certain policeman, lord of this dungeon. It costs me five *soles* to free my jailbird and I have to leave my ID as proof that I'll return. And there he is, my fake boyfriend.

"I thought you wouldn't come," he says, and he greets me with a kiss.

We walk arm in arm through Jirón de la Unión—the prison's version of the main street in downtown Lima that bears the same name. We have to dodge spit and I have to hold tight to my skirt because the prisoners are in the habit of stepping on women's skirts to pull them down. Calambrito is scrawny and has the face of a feral child. Sometimes he gets convulsions, hence the nickname Calambrito, or "muscle spasm." Our tour begins at the most dangerous block, which houses members of the Los Destructores and Los Elegantes gangs. Calambrito was assigned to this block before he was sent to the Pit. I admit to him I'm feeling intimidated.

"Don't you worry. Visitors are respected here. Visitors are sacred."

We walk by block eleven—the most heavily armed block, according to my companion. Most of the men in that block are policemen turned criminals. When Calambrito tells me the block is often in a state of cross fire, I hide my notepad, afraid it might set someone off. In none of the blocks does Calambrito feel as at home as he does in block four, which houses prisoners from the district of La Victoria, his old neighborhood. He was transferred out of block four after a fight, but his brothers still live there. I'm surprised by how clean the place is. There are restaurants, warehouses, and a salsa group is rehearsing in the yard. I start moving toward the band, but Calambrito already has a plan for us: the bar. There's a bar in here? Yes, with all the bells and whistles. On each table there's a bottle of *chicha de jora*, corn beer. We settle down for a chat. By his third glass, Calambrito is telling me about the time he killed two security guards point-blank. But let's not get off track: I'm not writing this to tell murderous tales, but to document the biography of his skin. His right shoulder sports the name "Grace" inside a heart pierced by an arrow on one side and flanked by a wing on the other.

"I was shot by her arrow, but then she left me so I added a wing."

On his other arm, Calambrito has another heart, this one bearing his mother's name, "Délida." It's a heart with thorns, a wounded heart. "My mother always gave me everything she could and I was never able to do the same for her." Tears roll down his cheeks and he wipes them off with his grimy hands. He says nobody visits him, that this morning he sent a message to his mother asking her to please come. But there's no use.

"Do you dance?"

It's not my first choice of a place to dance, but we get up and sway to one of those salsa songs that're danced up close. There's a unicorn under the heart-shaped tattoo on his right shoulder. It hardens on his muscle when I take him by the arm. He tells me the unicorn tattoo was given to him by his father, who died from a shot to the head. His dad was also a thief, and he spent his whole youth in Lurigancho. He was known as Cabaíto, "little horse," because of his equine face. By the time Calambrito got the unicorn tattoo, he was already a delinquent, and had been glassed on his arm after running into trouble. "Come here, I'm going to cover that scar up for you," his father had said. "I'm going to give you a tattoo so that you're my pony, my pony son. I'm a horse, but you're a unicorn." Calambrito also has a demon dragon on his back. It represents the Devil, he explains, because he's never been able to change. His two kids died in a fire at home while he was out getting drunk. His pain is a wound that will never heal.

Calambrito turns serious and explains to me that prisoners die from a lack of emotional support: "Not all women are the same. There are women who are after something, and then there are the true companions." I'm the kind who's after something, that much is clear. Then he tells me not to feel awkward, but that he's written me a poem. He hands me a scrap of paper with a G for Gabriela on the back: "*Gracias*—I'm thankful this life has led me to meet such a wonderful woman." I'd been warned that it was common practice to reel visitors in with poems, tears, and stories as a way to extract money from them. Although I was flattered, I didn't have a penny left. At each block I'd had to give out a coin, like a clueless tourist. We left as the orchestra was playing "Señora ley," but by then I'd had enough of salsa and was running late to my next meeting.

Reluctantly, Calambrito agrees to walk me to block seven. He knows that's where I'll leave him. The place is known as the Sheraton, the five-star wing of Lurigancho, where legend has it that a can of beer costs fifteen *soles*. The block houses gringos, Africans, Israelis, and Chinese men who've been on the front pages of newspapers. "Welcome to the mafia," says Calambrito. He's referring to the drug mules—people who got locked up for trafficking drugs, and probably then carried on trafficking from within the jail. The block has a giant TV screen, a well-equipped gym, a pool table, and, more important, José Richie, the tattoo artist.

Although he lives in block five, José Richie spends his days here with his clients, the posh prisoners. The tattoo artist is tall and his body is the product of daily exercise and a very unprisonlike diet. He seems honest, or is at least very good at feigning honesty. He is the polar opposite of the malnourished, sickly, and debauched Calambrito. Before I can introduce them, Richie tells me my "boyfriend" can't come into his block. So I say goodbye to my by-now old friend, who before leaving asks for another *sol*. I agree to meet him at the Pit in a couple of hours and I watch him walk away with what's left of the corn beer hidden in a black plastic bag.

The tattoo artist leads me to his cell, which looks like the room of an upper-middle-class bachelor, except it's behind bars. Black furniture, posters on the walls, television, DVD player. He's already spent five years in prison since the day he was caught with a box of floor tiles full of cocaine in the front seat of his Volkswagen—a gift from the cartel Los Africanos when he was their driver. Richie still claims he's innocent and ended up in jail because he was naive. But he's sure there's more to this than just bad luck. When Fujimori was in power, he tells me, capturing the Los Africanos cartel was a tactical gambit of the government's so-called war on drugs. The supposed manager of the floor tile factory double-crossed the cartel. Richie says the manager was really Montesinos, Fujimori's shady intelligence adviser and accomplice in the corruption scandals of his latter years in office.

On the day he realized that prison would be his home for an unspecified period of time, Richie tattooed his own bicep with a demon-faced gargoyle, its legs wrapped around a high-tension cable. He also inscribed his bicep with the phrase "no drugs" to make sure nothing like this happens to him again. "I'm making my way through hell without getting burned," he chants. Today Richie is the perfect, straight-edged inmate.

He's been studying the Bible for months, he exercises, eats fruit and vegetables, never hangs out at Jirón de la Unión, and every woman who visits him falls in love. He is the only tattoo artist in the prison to work in near-surgical conditions of cleanliness. In prisons, the risk of contracting AIDS through tattoo needles is very high. Richie realized that by offering "death-free tattoos" he could keep busy, express his artistic side, and earn a bit of cash. He shows me his homemade machine, built precariously out of a radio motor and a pen nib. His inspiration and designs come from magazines such as *Tattoo*. He says he wants to make them look like the inmates had them done at a professional studio, rather than in prison. When I talk about his stylistic choices he becomes very serious. If he inks a design, it must be inspired by the client's personality and have artistic nuance. He would never tattoo hearts, Christs, or mothers' names. He's a self-declared critic of the stick-and-poke tattoo, the kind that Calambrito's body is covered in. Never. Ever.

"They'll regret it afterward. They won't always want to be ex-cons."

It's late by now and we go for a walk around block seven in search of his friends. In the yard, I bump into the famous Arnie, an Israeli model who got locked up for cocaine possession. He flashes a catwalk smile my way. My guide tells me that a few days ago he tattooed a Star of David on Arnie's arm. Now we go up to the room of two Austrian prisoners. One of them looks like a singer from a boy band. They have a poster of the star of *Terminator* on the wall, to inspire their morning weight-lifting sessions. The tattoos on their arms are the work of world-class tattoo guru Claus Fuhrmann. Or at least that's what they say. And I have to admit they're impressive. *"Bribón"* (rascal), I read on one of their stomachs. And a message on the other's leg sums up his lifestyle: *"Sin dolor no hay juego,"* no pain, no game.

But the game's over for me. It's nearly five o'clock, time to get out of here for those of us who can, and I still need to find Calambrito to get my ID back. Richie only accompanies me as far as the entrance to Jirón de la Unión. He's forbidden himself from going to that "contaminating place." He pulls out some money and calls out: "Hey, Camina Rico, take her to twenty." Camina Rico is an ageless creature who swings his hips as he walks, like he's dancing. We cross the yard and get to block twenty, but there's no sign of Calambrito. That's what I get for trusting an assassin. The policeman doesn't want to give me back my documents and I don't have any money left to bribe him with. I return to block four with Camina Rico, but Calambrito is not there either. I see a familiar face:

"Have you seen Calambrito?"

"Saw him earlier. He was with his mom."

"With his mom?"

I go back to block twenty to beg the policeman for my ID because they're about to lock the doors. He finally agrees. But before handing it to me, he writes down the name of the convict I paid five *soles* to get out of here, as if making a point that he was signing Calambrito's death sentence. I hope that he really is with his mom, drunk, happy, and hiding in some less grim corner of the prison, even if he'll have to pay for his escapade later. I walk to the prison's main gate and I'm stopped by Major Véliz, who tries to soften the desolate panorama: it's his birthday, and to commemorate such an important date, the men in the Pit will be forgiven and sent back to their blocks.

On my way out, I bump into Colonel Pantaleón Valdivia. I finally dare to ask if he's read the novel by Vargas Llosa. He says only part of it, but he can attest to it all being true. He saw it all himself when he was sent to the jungle. I say goodbye and become part of the battalion of women who exit the prison alone. They all hold out their arms to the swarm of children who stand outside holding cotton balls soaked in rubbing alcohol. In exchange for a few coins, the children wipe off the numbers the guards had written on these women's arms—the stigma, the evidence of their history with an outlaw. I won't allow them to erase mine.

PLANET SWINGERS

TONIGHT I INTEND TO BE UNFAITHFUL—with my husband's permission. 6&9's entrance is so discreet that we've walked past it twice. I'm wearing a coat and the three beers I drank earlier tonight—that's what it took to get me to leave the house in this skimpy outfit. Jaime has a four-day stubble and looks so handsome and so mine that I can't fathom him going to bed with someone who isn't me in a few minutes. It's eleven o'clock on a Thursday night in Barcelona. The TV above the bar is playing a porn film in which a truck driver slams a brittle blonde.

"Is this your first time here?"

"Yes."

"Come with me," the hostess says.

The night promises to be intergenerational, multi-racial, and multi-orgasmic. Unlike other clubs that attract rich sixty-year-olds on the decline, 6&9 is popular for catering to youngsters at the height of their sexual appetite. It's also renowned for being "hygienic," a commendation I'd initially dismissed due to my belief, to paraphrase Woody Allen, that sex is only done right if it's dirty, but which ended up tipping the balance in its favor.

Once inside, our hostess gives us a tour and explains the rules of the game. "This is the warm-up room," she says, "where you can grab a drink and catch a bit of the movie or have a dance." We descend into an erotic version of Plato's cave. "Clothes aren't allowed from here on. You can get the keys to a locker from the bar." She needlessly points out the room's impressive centerpiece: a hundred-foot, L-shaped bed that regularly creaks under the weight of fifty couples or so, though at this hour it's still deserted. "We've got condom dispensers, to the right is the Jacuzzi, further along there's showers for couples, and then we've got the dark-room, a kind of nudist mini-disco. If you're ever not interested in a person just tap them on the shoulder."

That's the password. Each club has their own polite way for clients to inform others of their boundaries.

"And what's this room for?" I ask. It's the orgy room, where anything goes.

I glance sideways at Jaime.

I've been here for an hour and the only thing I've swapped is a cigarette. We're supposed to try and hook up with other couples, but all we've done so far is look around.[1]

I'd spent a whole afternoon getting ready, like a bride for her wedding night, and had followed the club's instructions duti-fully: "Women, wear sexy clothes." I squished myself into a tiny black pleated miniskirt.[2] I wore a low-cut blouse and a pair of

---

[1] The year after *Sexografías* was published, a Spanish publisher commissioned me to write an entire book on swingers. I spent a year visiting clubs—from the seediest to the most sophisticated—meeting couples in bars and proposing exchanges, having sex with strangers, men and women, always with Jaime at my side. I wound up feeling so sick of that world of bodily transactions that I became polyamorous. Polyamorists are not polygamous and are the complete opposite of swingers, because the agreement between those involved allows for love in addition to sex.
[2] The experience of keeping your partner waiting while you get ready to have sex with someone else is an interesting one.

knee-high boots that made my thighs look appetizing. I opted for a Brazilian wax. When I showed it to Jaime, he, seeing how explicit my intentions were, seemed to finally take in what we were about to do.

The loftier swingers claim that by relating genitally to others under the watchful gaze of their partners, they avoid succumbing to secretive affairs. I'm intrigued by this shared adventure, this sexual freedom that emerges from consent. This supervised adultery.

Although we had never set foot in a club like this one, Jaime and I could be considered an open-minded couple. Admittedly I've contributed to our credentials more than he has. I first had sex when I was sixteen (nothing unusual there). That same year, I had my first threesome (with my boyfriend and a female friend). Soon after, I had my first threesome with two completely unknown men (and with that same boyfriend as a witness). I know it's no world record, but it's enough for card-carrying liberals not to brush me aside. After five years together, Jaime and I can count among our experiences one frustrated partner-swapping episode and several threesomes, although always with another woman. As for jealousy, if he falls in love with another woman or has a crush on someone, I get possessive. But jealousy for him is more tied up with sex: if another man touches me, he wants to break their face.[3]

---

3 I'm afraid I'm going to start talking about methodology. The only way to be loyal to the spirit of this story is to allow myself to be guided by chance rather than by facts, to go with the flow of situations and of people in a way that I wouldn't be able to if I presented myself as a journalist. To expose the life and experience of

Before coming here, Jaime was willing to go along with it, and seemed to be taking our planned swinger incursion as a healthy adventure. He was prepared to take the plunge and allow me to go as far as I wanted to, although he preferred not to dwell on the details. For me, our expedition was more of a settling of scores (like I mentioned, we'd only ever had threesomes with women). Although I trusted in Jaime's adventurous spirit, I was worried there might be some last-minute backpedaling. A person can never be sure how open-minded they truly are until they find themselves alongside couples who practice freedom and excess so unrestrainedly. According to the swinger code of conduct, backing out halfway is for closed-minded, insecure couples—an unforgivable insult to any self-respecting modern couple.

It's midnight and some thirty couples have settled into the hookup room. It's clear that some are not only here to flirt, but to exhibit their merchandise and hopefully stage a porno of their own.[4] There are withdrawn and intimidated couples, finicky couples who scrutinize any man or woman who walk in the door, and

---

swingers, I should first expose my own intimacy. To put into view, warts and all, not only my own nakedness, fears, complexes, and jealousy, but also my fantasies and my morbid curiosity. Let's just say if I was going to get involved in their lives I had to follow it through to the end, so that everything I was going to say about swingers would also be true about myself. You'd be right to point out that this piece is more about me than it is about swingers.

4 Swingers' penchant for exhibitionism appeared before me in its fullest expression when we visited the Club de Pedralbes, also in Barcelona. Maradona had lived there during his good streak with Barça, so having sex there held an additional, morbid fascination, especially in the spectacular indoor swimming pool, where half a dozen stunning, sculptural couples displayed their sexual proficiency and put to shame any commoner that dared show up.

libidinous ones who undress you with their eyes. Others simply watch, perhaps because they have no other choice. Jaime and I feel ridiculous, and that's considering we're still dressed. Most people are becoming increasingly touchy-feely. I start to feel scared of this abstract entity, this anonymous "swinger couple" that might approach us. The tension is so palpable that Jaime and I don't even feel like kissing each other. The snobbishness of being a swinger is killing me. I want to take refuge in love, our couch, domesticity. But this existential trance is interrupted by a migratory wave of couples heading for the nudist zone, the land of bartering. Jaime and I exchange one last complicit glance before going down the stairs leading to the lockers in the basement.

We hesitate before taking off our clothes in the middle of a brightly lit corridor, alongside a chubby-cheeked, naked older couple. The pensioners pay us no attention, though, and their bodies, which have already seen the rise and fall of the empire of the senses, disappear into the darkness.[5] We opt to imitate the

---

5 The older couple is a chapter in itself in my swinger history. I've been titillated by the slightest brush of a wrinkly, veined hand, I must admit. I owe this particular affinity to *La misteriosa desaparición de la marquesita de Loria*, a lewd novella by José Donoso and one of my favorite reads as a teenager. In it, an octogenarian lawyer dies happily of a heart attack, shaken by the extraordinary orgasm torn from him by the tight vulva of La Marquesita, an aristocratic young woman who has just been widowed and is his client. I can't think of a better way to die. I've masturbated many times to the magnificent description of the moment when the smell of the old geezer meets the fresh breath of La Marquesita's pubis. In my nights of partner swapping in a swingers' club, I saw many a couple that could have been my grandparents or even my great-grandparents. One night, I notice a woman over sixty, still beautiful, with long, blond hair. While she shows Jaime and me her tongue from across the room, she strokes one of her sagging breasts. Her bald, slightly hunched partner—husband? lover? dominoes buddy?—stands next to her. Soon, the woman is devouring Jaime on a sofa. It's like watching *Taboo 1*

more conservative couples and wrap ourselves in white towels. Everyone looks at us, the fresh meat. We walk past the Jacuzzi, which judging by the steam and moaning must be home to Lucifer himself. On the superbed, about ten couples kiss and caress, some patiently, others noisily approaching climax. I'm disappointed sex is only happening in duos. Since we've just arrived, we can't tell if what we see on the bed is the product of exchanges or not. Perhaps none of the couples rolling around are in their original configurations.

After a brief recon loop, we realize that the real party seems to be taking place in a cave separated off by some curtains.

---

live. It's all smiles until I realize my mistake. The woman's venerable companion is coming toward me, oddly, on all fours. He is moving slowly, as if giving me the chance to escape. Jaime is nostalgically suckling on the old woman. I fight him over one of her nipples. It's a free ride into the past. But I pay dearly for my distraction. I feel at the other end of me an undesirable suction, as if a jellyfish had stuck to me. The granddad is on his knees licking my crotch. I try to concentrate, to enjoy the concrete fact of clitoral stimulation, even though it's somewhat clumsy, and I push his warm, downy head toward me. I can't believe it. He's reverent, docile, toothless. Not even the family cocker spaniel, who so many times tasted me with his kilometric tongue on those mornings of adolescent solitude, made me feel this tender. To avoid being a bad-mannered granddaughter, I reciprocate by taking his penis, but I realize that the venerable old man either doesn't know Viagra exists, or not even that works for him anymore. With the greatest respect, I put it back where I found it. Then he leans over me, introduces one of his fingers, and pulls out and goes back in with uncharacteristic energy. I realize that what he lacks in firmness elsewhere he makes up for with a strong and vehement right arm. We go on like that for nearly ten minutes, with no variation. Each time I manage to get him off me he runs to his wife like a wounded child. She, on the other hand, is an unmovable beast. Each time the lady brushes him off to concentrate on my husband, the gentleman starts drilling me again with his finger. If he carries on like that something's going to tear. "I'm going to get a drink," I say to them, and turn to look at them one last time: the lady devouring Jaime and the man who could do nothing but masturbate me watches me walk—his last chance to die with a bang.

Eight couples in towels are dancing in the half-light while the temperature rises out of control. They give themselves over to the game, although they still haven't swapped anything. I can't decide if I'm ready to have sex in front of so many people, but then my impatience explodes and I decide to let loose by giving Jaime a few minutes of homely and devoted oral sex, shielded in the darkness but aware of the exhibitionism of my act. Other couples draw near to watch, and then follow suit. I've always wanted to be a sexual agitator and this is, without a doubt, my fifteen minutes of fame. Jaime receives my initiative eagerly. The towels slip down to our feet.

This initiation into Swingerland has been pretty good so far. I feel like I've garnered some sort of notoriety, and the group has let loose thanks to my good deed. Or at least that's my fantasy. I start to live it out: I believe that our peers have started to look at me lasciviously. I find myself in the arms of a bald and impetuous man. His wife stands in front of me and begins that little faux lesbian dance that men like so much. I follow her lead—what the hell. She's beautiful and very slim, she's sweaty and, to be honest, looks like she's on Ecstasy. It's as if an appreciative octopus were touching us; everyone is gently pushing us together. The wave of desire propagates itself. But who is this guy who won't let go of my tits? Is it the same bald guy or is it someone else? Impossible to tell. I look for Jaime and I see him with Ecstasy Girl, also groping with abandon. I feel a slight burn, but nothing serious. I imagine he must feel the same.

I'm relieved to see he's having fun and isn't worried about me, or at least that he's pretending convincingly. I'm going around from arm to arm and discover I like to feel this way, anonymous, at the mercy of whims bigger than myself. I start a solitary game that involves insolently pawing at the couples who haven't joined in yet. They give me dirty looks that almost shatter my fantasy. Maybe I'm unknowingly breaking some swinger rule. I can't find Jaime among the anonymous bodies; I feel anxious, I begin to think I've lost him, if not forever then at least for tonight. But then a hand pushes through the ridiculous curtains and drags me out.

The word "swinger" alludes to ease of movement—in this case the movement in question takes place from one bed to another. I've spoken to more than half a dozen swinger couples tonight and they've all told me that swinging is a sure antidote against infidelity. They call this a new kind of sexuality, capable of saving dying marriages. "Sexual fidelity," a woman tells me, "is the false god of closed marriage." They believe life as a couple is enriched by playing away from home now and then. But the antidote often becomes a poison, and some confess to me that they have become hooked on someone else's partner and even started to see them secretly. There are even gross cases of breach of contract that turn into four-way marriages. Love, it seems, is still a minefield.

Georges Bataille used to say it's a mistake to think that marriage has little to do with eroticism just because it's the conventional, legitimized territory on which we play out our sexuality.[6] The forbidden might be more exciting, but bodies tend to

---

6 To write about swingers, I considered Bataille and Sade's writings on orgies and the erotic. I didn't want to write a steamy article about sex that would get my readers off—I wanted to come up with a grand, pretentious theory about swingers. I wanted to hide behind erudite quotes and pompous declarations that were, of course, quickly detected and weeded out by my editors.

understand each other better over time. If a union is furtive, pleasure cannot become organized and remains elusive. Habit has the power to satisfy what impatience overlooks. To swingers, marriage is unthinkable without sex parties, clubs, and an occasional orgy. Before coming here, I envisioned 6&9 as a temple of pleasure and sophistication in the style of Kubrick's last film. But what happens at a swingers club barely resembles the scenes of glamour and lust that people imagine from the outside. To begin with, it's full of sweaty, potbellied men, and women with breast implants. It also isn't the spectacle of equality that swingers would have us believe—that world full of rampant sexuality, shared fantasies, and low divorce rates. Some studies show that divorce is actually more common among open couples.

The hand that's holding mine is Jaime's, of course. After the virulence of the dark room, I follow him to the superbed. We want a moment of peace and intimacy. We begin to caress each other, but I can't concentrate at all. Jaime, on the other hand, is already on top of me, very eager. I ask him what he'd thought. Nothing special, he didn't like Ecstasy Girl's porn star mannerisms. I'm surprised by my success and whisper into his ear, showing off:

"Were you jealous?"

"Very."

"But did you enjoy seeing me with someone else?"

"I'd rather avoid it for as long as I live."

I say what I always say, that seeing him with someone else excites me as much as it hurts me. We make love. Without realizing it, we're behaving like typical swingers: we've been extramaritally stimulated and now we're consummating sex conjugally. From time to time, I look to my right and to my left, curious about our bedfellows. To my right, there's a couple of kids who can't be more than twenty-five. He's giving her clumsy oral sex. The older couple on my left, both of them very fat, are visual representations of the weight of habit. She's on top and doesn't skip a beat until she comes. Maybe custom is the most efficient stimulator. But then Jaime starts thrusting with fury, and my musings give way to a long orgasm.

We take a break and a cold shower. In the lounge, we meet a very friendly couple. He's a truck driver and she's a nurse. Jaime says the woman reminds him of his elementary school math teacher. She's wearing glasses and has enormous tits. I think it would be a nice fantasy to do it with your math teacher. I already said I'm not jealous. Her husband looks like the Gingerbread Man. He's short, stocky, and has a deeply creased face. The four of us step into the Jacuzzi.

Should we do it with the first couple kind enough to talk to us? We are faced with a scenario that is very common in this world: Jaime is interested in the math teacher with the enormous tits, while I can't conceive of having sex with the Gingerbread Man, and I'd rather go find the bald man and Ecstasy Girl and finish what we'd started. In these cases, according to the swinger handbook, it's better to abort your mission: otherwise the swinger club might turn into a fight club.

"Don't even think about it," I say to Jaime when at last we're alone. The couple has gone off to dance in the dark room, surely thinking we'd follow them. I don't like the teacher's husband, what can I do, although I'm disappointed to discover I'm not as democratic as I thought. We flee like cowards to the orgy room, a good place to hide. Savoring our nascent "swingerism," we watch as two couples perform a partner swap with an air of having done this countless times before.

The other side of the room has a smaller bed that holds several panting, splayed bodies. The word "couple" no longer makes any sense. There's no way to distinguish individual bodies—this is just one huge entity. Maybe it's the goddess Kali, but instead of several hands she seems to have sprouted several penises. The moans tell us we've arrived too late, but we still try to participate. Two very beautiful couples seem to be having a great time nearby.

Is this a private orgy or are we welcome to join? A woman is masturbating a guy while another guy penetrates her. Both men stop, get up from the bed, and pin her against the wall. The attack is vigorous, there is a beastly component to it. Jaime and I are mute observers of the marvels of nature, but above all of the marvels of culture. This scene deconstructs another swinger-scene myth: that of equal opportunities. Here, as in the real world, the people who succeed are beautiful and sensual, they work out and get plastic surgery. Those who don't must resign themselves to onanism.

"Look who it is," says Jaime. Yes, the math teacher and the Gingerbread Man are heading our way. Once they've reached us, she starts sucking her husband off and then straddles him, swaying her supertits and riding gently. Jaime reaches his hands out to the teacher's breasts while I go down on him again. Gingerbread Man exercises his right and stretches his hands out toward me. He grabs my tits, and I grab his wife's. We all grab the teacher's tits. I ride the man deliberately facing away from him and end up face to face with the teacher, who is being humped by Jaime from behind. Gingerbread Man masturbates me with his truck driver fingers until I come. I feel grateful for so many displays of disinterested love. Once everyone's satisfied, we part ways without saying goodbye.

Several days have passed since I lost my swinger virginity. I rewind the tape and travel for a moment back to that world of sexual exchanges. I see those needy of pleasure being exploited by multinationals and their tentacles, the so-called alchemists of sex offering artificial paradises, fake fountains of eternal youth, and other palliatives against unhappiness. I see marriages on the edge of collapse, frigid women, elderly people, drug addicts, cokeheads beyond recall, good Catholics, the dispossessed of Viagra, premature ejaculators, micropenises, dictators, impotents, presidents of the free world, the working class in general; all swingers with their days numbered living out the last throes of desire as an infernal journey toward desperation.

It's a stiflingly hot Friday night in Barcelona and Jaime is asleep in front of the TV while I type away frantically. It's a hassle, this business of discovering new pleasures. One always wants more of them. Paradoxically, though, swinging destroyed my claim to sexual open-mindedness. I'd traveled the swingerverse and then betrayed their primary rule: never talk about swinging. Maybe I was never really open-minded enough.

ADVICE FROM AN UNYIELDING
DOMINATRIX TO A BEWILDERED DISCIPLE

MONIQUE IS SITTING on a blood-red leather couch. I spy from afar as a masked and naked man with a chain around his neck insistently kisses the tip of her boot. She strokes his head as if he were some kind of pet or circus animal, and then gives him a kick on the chin. One of Monique's eyes is as gelid as the eye of a fish. Her other eye looks at everything with infinite contempt. Including me. When she spots me, she recognizes me and smiles bitterly. She has the ability to make you feel like a cockroach about to be crushed under one of her high heels.

I'm at the Barcelona International Erotic Film Festival because a magazine has asked me to cover Club Bizarre's star act—the fearsome Lady Monique de Nemours, who belonged to the select group of dominatrixes inducted to the Other World Kingdom (OWK), a world that used to be located in a sixteenth-century castle in Černá, Czech Republic, and was visited by rich business-men who took time off from pulling the levers of global politics to be subjected by women to extreme cruelties. At the OWK, women, spearheaded by the professional dominatrix Queen Patricia I, ruled supreme. Men were little more than farm animals, inferior creatures at the service of women. When they were not being auctioned off like a painting, the dominatrixes often used them as race horses. Monique is the only Spanish dominatrix who was granted citizenship to this micronation.

Gaining access to such an illustrious figure is no easy task, least of all just as she's about to begin a session and people are gathering at the door of Club Bizarre waiting to witness some live scenes of pain.

"I wanted to ask you a favor . . . " I manage to say to Monique, who is advancing to the second floor followed by a consort of men on their knees, whose testicles are bound with rope and metal rings.

"What?"

"Could you hit me?" She stops for a few seconds, glares at me and gives a chortle.

"I don't dominate women," she says categorically, before disappearing into the crowd.

Resigned, I take my place at the end of the line and hope that I'll get a seat in the auditorium.

Lady Monique and I have met once before. A week ago, I went by her studio to interview her. It was not a pleasant experience.

"Are you the journalist?" I turn around and recognize one of Monique's bodyguards. They're both there. Muscular and wearing matching black shirts and shades.

"Monique says you should come with us."

I'd prepared for the interview and arrived early to meet Monique, but my excitement soon turned into despair. To begin with, I waited for at least an hour. When she finally arrived, she was accompanied by a man and a dog. Dominatrixes usually have one or more slaves at their disposal. And I say slave in the full sense of the word. They aren't necessarily lovers, they are usually people who feel privileged to service someone like Lady Monique. The slave excused himself, explaining that he needed to take Monique's clothes to the laundry. We entered her dungeon, which was an apartment in a building like any other. I wondered what the dominatrix's neighbors must think of her. On the ground floor was the BDSM studio, the place where she officiated sessions for which she charged five hundred euros. Younger dominatrixes rent out the space from time to time for their own sessions. Its two stories are full of objects and accessories: a bondage wheel, a St. Andrew's cross, a spanking bench, a stretching table, a water-play den, an iron cage, a bondage chair, and suspension gear. As she gave me a quick tour I kept asking what everything was, like a toddler learning to speak.

I'd hoped that Monique would help me understand the physical side of sadism, but the interview couldn't have gotten off to a worse start. I'd forgotten my recorder and was taking notes by hand. Monique was appalled, and immediately became defensive. Each question I asked seemed to her impertinent and stupid, so she decided to ask me the questions instead. Her goal was obviously to delegitimize me: Where was I from? Was I really a journalist? What swamp had I crawled out of?

She was showing me no mercy, taking advantage of my evident inexperience. Monique started sizing up my knowledge of BDSM, and soon realized that I was no expert on the subject. She was so furious that she started yelling—she could not believe that my boss, a personal friend of hers, would send her such an inept journalist. I genuinely considered leaving, but I took a deep breath and charged again.

"What do you make of all the cases of violence against women that we see every day on the Spanish news?" I asked with my most socially concerned face.

"Each time it happens, I admire myself more."

"Do you think men might come to your studio to redeem themselves?"

"You'd have to interview them. That's a personal matter, but as far as I know, I don't have women batterers here. If I heard otherwise, they wouldn't be able to get out of here fast enough."

Listening to Monique, I remember each piece of shit who has ever hurt me, and at last I understand the crusade of the army of dominatrixes. I feel like putting on leather clothes and having a tormented man beg me for mercy. I want him under my boot and I want to use him as a rug.

I follow the bodyguards as we thread our way through the crowd. Club Bizarre contains a stage, a bar, and a dozen tables and chairs for the guests. Low lighting and a funeral march set the atmosphere. The two bodyguards show me to a front-row table beside the stage.

"Monique says that if you want her to dominate you, you can offer yourself as a volunteer during the session."

"Okay," I say. My original idea, which I'd already thought was quite risky, was for her to take me to the women's toilet or some backstage room and whip me. Something anecdotal, cute, the kind of thing one writes in the intro to an article to be funny. Getting up on stage to be flagellated in public was something else entirely. Why had Monique betrayed her principle of not dominating women and invited me to become a part of the show?

On the stage, the torture machines glint under the light reflectors. The first slave is already tied to a cross. Monique emerges with another slave, who is wearing a dog's collar. He is not wearing a mask. The audience is silent. Monique is suited up in black latex, fuchsia tights, gloves, and a pair of razor-sharp stiletto boots. The ritual begins with Monique lightly caressing the slave's penis before issuing him a severe lash of the whip. The slave looks like a marathon-running granddad. I don't know whether to laugh or cry. He's flaccid, wiry, and passive. All in all, pretty pathetic. He does not have an erection, not even close. It's hard to believe he's having a good time, but he is. Pleasure doesn't have to be visible. I must admit, though, I still can't understand the attraction.

My experience of sadism is very different. I suppose I'm more versed in psychological abuse. I've felt pleasure debasing; winning an argument; imposing myself with reason; making fun of habits, appearance, and dreams; manipulating; and exploiting for my own gain—but I've never tied or beat anyone up. My idea of sadomasochism until then had been closer to the image of the stunning Bettie Page lashing her submissive women. I'd thought erotic humiliation was about beautiful people dressed in latex. Not this.

Monique grabs a candle and pours the boiling wax on the man's chest; he shudders slightly. In the end, she pours a few drops on his glans. There's a gasp from the audience. The following number consists of practicing bondage on the slave's bruised penis. Monique is weaving a knot of ropes that turns the slave's member a purplish color. People applaud. I don't. I'm frightened. I'm shaking. I feel sorry. Not for that ball of flesh, but for myself.

"Is there a volunteer who would like to come up to the stage and feel my whip?" Monique's voice is mellifluous, even sweet. I can see that her lazy eye is twinkling in the dark. She means me. She's calling me.

Anyone interested in being dominated by Lady Monique must first fill in an extensive questionnaire, which includes a section about any health issues. She needs to know if you're willing to be marked, what clothes you prefer her to wear, if you're okay with a dog's collar, a harness, or a chastity belt. Do you prefer mummification or leather belts? Do you want to expiate your sins or be used for the pleasure of Lady Monique? A dog, a goddess's sexual slave, a torturer's victim, a nurse's patient, a prisoner faced with a violent interrogator, or a naughty schoolchild at the hands of an unyielding governess? Humiliation, equestrian training, golden showers, enemas, or fisting? Do you lick feet, boots, pussy, anus? Do you like being slapped? Do you enjoy hot wax, ice, scratches, sensory deprivation, or electrostimulation? Everything must be made explicit.

"I'm 5'5" and weigh a little over a hundred pounds," she says to me. She stands and we measure each other up. I can't believe she's only that tall. But her real superiority is not physical. It's intuition, tact, eroticism.

"Show me some tricks of the trade. What do I have to do if I want to be a dominatrix? What instruments is it best to start with?"

"It doesn't matter whether you start with your nails, teeth, words, or a wooden spoon—anything will do. There are no hard and fast rules. This is wide open, you can play with anything your imagination allows. Some people don't like marks and others do, some people like the riding crop but don't enjoy the whip, some people prefer a hairbrush."

Monique seems happy to share her secrets. She's starting to feel comfortable with her new, obedient disciple.

"What did you start with?"

"I started with needles, because I like to be extreme. With needles and clamps. You put them on their chest, nipples, testicles, penis."

"What do I need to know before using the needles?"

"I wouldn't recommend you start with needles. I studied dermatology, so I knew what I was doing. Do you know anything about medicine?"

"No."

"Then don't do it. You need to know where to pierce. This isn't just a silly game. You're playing with their intelligence and their body. If you tie their arms above their head, you have to make sure their blood flow reaches the tips of their fingers, make sure those hands don't get shaky and purple. You can't tie a person to a cross and leave them there for more than fifteen or twenty minutes unless they have great circulation. You need to check if their pressure is high or low."

"Do you set limits?"

"They vary by person. I like to use the bondage wheel with people who have already tried other things. There are people who get off from being on the cross. Others don't need much; it's enough to say 'come here, kneel before me.'"

"How's your clientele?"

"The Iberian macho is absolutely clueless, he thinks BDSM is harm, pain, blood. They won't be giving me a plaque in a park anytime soon, but I hope I'm opening peoples' minds."

"When did you discover this was your thing?"

"Since kindergarten, when I would go around getting into fights with boys in vacant lots. I started with my partner. It was a game we later combined with sex in whatever way we wanted."

"Can a dominatrix cry in public?"

"Why not? I cried in public when I was inducted to the OWK and when I was given the title of 'Queen of Spades' at the Club Bizarre of the Barcelona International Erotic Film Festival. Of course you can cry."

"But I guess you shouldn't bite your nails," I say, and show her my nails bitten down to the quick.

"Biting your nails is a terrible act of weakness. It signals insecurity and nervousness, a lack of self-control. You can't be nervous while placing a clamp and a needle," she tells me, calling over her dog.

"What breed is she?"

"She's a boxer. She's called Switch. She won't cross the street without me telling her to. The more I get to know people, the more I love my dog," she says.

"Are men like dogs?"

"I'd compare them to other animals, or things. Some are dumb as a chair, a lamppost, a table. Others can be used to feast your senses. Hearing a 'thank you, my lady' after the thwack of my whip is, the devotion with which they kiss my hands, hearing or seeing them ask permission to greet me—it's out of this world.

I haven't lain a finger on them and they're already trembling. There's nothing bloodthirsty in it. I'm sophisticatedly cruel, bitterly attentive."

"Do I need to have sex with my slave?"

"I don't have sex with the slaves. In general, a dominatrix will have sex only if she wants to. The slave has to really earn it."

"And do you have to be a dominatrix twenty-four hours a day?"

"I'm a person twenty-four hours a day. My character is always the same."

Lady Monique didn't have a slave at hand to play our guinea pig that night, so for my practical lesson we pretended that the corner of a piece of furniture was the tip of a penis.

LESSON 1

HOW TO WHIP THE VIRILE MEMBER WITH RIGOR AND ELEGANCE

Monique ordered me to take the riding crop. I managed to issue a swift whip on the imaginary penis. "Work on your wrist movement," said Monique. "Well done, you're doing great. Now imagine that these are his nipples."

LESSON 2

HOW TO DELIVER WELL-AIMED LASHES

She gave me a rod and asked me to remove the clamps she'd placed on the piece of furniture with one blow. The idea was to learn to avoid tearing the skin.

LESSON 3
HOW TO FLOG

For this she handed me the flogger, a whip with a leather handle and several strips. "I want to see your grip. Test it on your hand." I took the flogger, combed it with my fingers and brought it down on my hand putting on a "bad girl" facial expression. Monique told me to flog the wardrobe. I hit so hard I thought I nearly dismantled it. Monique laughed at me. "If that was a slave you would've destroyed his kidneys. What matters is not to hit hard, it's to hit intoxicatingly."

They say cruelty is a purely feminine virtue. I looked at Monique and asked her what was the most essential thing for me to know.

"Believe in yourself, love yourself, and know that you're the best. You need to be self-aware, honorable, know your limits, and know the human body. Otherwise, it's like handing a revolver to a monkey."

I get up and, possessed by masochism, make my way to the stage. Monique whispers to me:

"Strip down to your panties and bra."

"Umm, can I keep my skirt on?"

Her bodyguards place me in the center of the stage. I'm paralyzed with stage fright more than I am with any fear of pain. Monique talks to the audience, tells them who knows what, but she's talking about me, of that I'm sure. Probably that I'm submissive and that she's going to flog me. Because of the lights, I fortunately can't see the crowd. The slave and his livid balls are still squatting on the stage.

"Take off your shirt," says Monique with a ritual gesture. I do. "Are you afraid?" she whispers in my ear. I say I'm not. She treats me with extreme delicacy. She tells me to go up to the bench and kneel. I'm wearing knee-high black boots, a miniskirt, and a bra. I realize my look is quite fetish. Monique lifts up my skirt, uncovering my small but firm ass and the little black thong chosen especially for my visit to the erotic film festival.

"What a nice little butt," Monique says in my ear. She strokes it tenderly. She gives it little pats, like a loving mother. I'd like to be in the audience to watch myself star in this spanking scene.

Am I turning anyone on? Monique caresses me again. She spanks me with one hand and strokes me with the other. It's like being in love. Intermittent pleasure and pain.

"Are you all right?" the woman "abusing" me asks sweetly. I turn to see what she's doing next with my ass. I can't help it. Now she picks up the famous cat-o'-nine-tails. She tests it on the palm of her hand, the way she taught me to do that time in her dungeon. One, two, three. She lets it fall on my ass. The first time is just a tickle. With the second and third blow the sensation is one of pleasant warmth. My ears are ringing, like every time someone tries to sell me something on the phone and use that polite and monotonous voice, or whenever something happens that I don't understand and can't control, and whose strangeness hypnotizes me pleasantly. That's how I feel now. Might this be masochistic pleasure?

My ass must be red by now, and I keep thinking this will be the last blow. But it's not. It continues, and now she flogs me with a vengeance.

I don't know if it's due to some experience from my child-hood, but disobedience and subsequent punishment are very ingrained in my character. Might I truly be the submissive woman Monique presented to the audience today?

In that instant of brief pain, what comes to mind are all those times I've practiced submission with my partners in bed. There is nothing like a bit of sadomasochism to yank a sexual relationship out of lethargy. Asking your partner to give you a slap is nothing unusual. It's quite common to tell them to hit you a little harder, a little stronger; to ask that they tell you off for being bad and give you what you deserve for being ungrateful. Men tend to respond to the challenge with potent spanks on the ass and furious blows. They strangle, slap, and gag—all the while excited at the fantasy that you're a bitch who must be taught a lesson. What they don't know is that it's not a fantasy, that you really are an evil bitch, and that they're unknowingly and rightfully taking revenge. Who is the domi-nated one then? I've pleasurably atoned for my hidden sadism by being tied up and receiving blows, but I'd never had a master until today.

I turn around to see what's next and Monique delivers a last well-aimed blow to my branded cheeks. She helps me up to my feet. The skin on my ass is pulsating and burning, but as I stagger away from the bench I "fall into subspace," which is what submissives call the state of trance that follows the acceptance of their passive condition. A powerful moment in which the submissive becomes pliable, amorous, and happy.

"Give her a round of applause," I hear Monique say, and I detect a tinge of mockery in the voice of my dominator.

The black-clad gorillas help me down the stairs, one at either side of me. My legs are still shaky. I glance at the audience one last time and return to my seat amidst the ovation. What the hell—amidst my ovation, *my* ovation.

TRANS

HE THOUGHT SHE WAS A GUY and she thought he was a girl. They'd met in their neighborhood and had starting seeing more of each other. One night, Melvin stayed over at Amelia's house.

She was sleeping and he wasn't, so he woke her up:

"You're not a man, are you?"

Amelia half-opened her eyes.

"And you're not a woman, so let me sleep." Melvin hugged her and they went back to sleep.

But neither of them knew what to make of this relationship. Amelia was a lesbian. And butch. And a virgin. She felt that being with Melvin, even though he had tits, was like being with a man. Melvin considered himself a feminine person, but at the end of the day he was still a man. He would meet Amelia in corners in the outskirts of Lima where she used to drink with her friends and get in fights with all the men who disrespected her.

"Hey, *papito*," Melvin would say to her, "I know you *look* like a man, but you're not a man, all right? You pick the fights but I'm the one who gets the black eye. I'm the husband here, for fuck's sake. Come on, let's go home."

In private, Melvin called Amelia "princess" and Amelia called Melvin "cowboy."

Whenever they got drunk together, Melvin would yell at her: "You're my woman. When I met you, you were a girl and I made you a woman."

I arrived in Paris this morning on a direct flight from Barcelona, with my phone dead and my tits bursting with milk. I've left my three-month-old baby at home but my tits don't seem to have gotten the memo: I'm worried they might explode at any moment. I feel so guilty for having left my daughter behind that I think this *in crescendo* discomfort is well-deserved punishment. It's the rush hour at Charles de Gaulle airport and they're making increasingly weird security announcements, things like "if you've got a shampoo bottle in your suitcase, you might get accused of fabricating liquid explosives." French phone cards suck. When Vanesa finally answers the phone, she sounds like she's just woken and has a terrible hangover. She turns up an hour later.

She'd offered to pick me up from the airport and let me stay in her apartment for the weekend. From what she said, everything was going great for her. She made a real point of telling me she had a car, an apartment, and that she spoke fluent French. She added that she was studying theater and worked "doing something online," which she'd explain to me later.

Vanesa identifies as trans, though she hasn't undergone sex reassignment surgery.

I'd met her four years ago at Kápital, the biggest nightclub in Comas, the populous district in northern Lima. Back then Vanesa was undoubtedly one of the belles of the ball, monopolizing the scene with her chiseled figure and a red wig that made her look like the girl from *The Fifth Element*. Soon after I met her, though, she crossed the pond like transgender Peruvians tend to do, and I didn't see her again until this morning.

From a distance, Vanesa looks exactly as she did four years ago, but up close something seems to have deteriorated or been lost forever. She's very thin and her bony, boyish face is almost entirely lost in her wet, messy hair. She isn't wearing makeup. She's in skinny jeans, white boots, and a white polo. Despite the cold, she isn't wearing a coat. She doesn't overdo things; I get the impression she's trying to look like an unremarkable woman. Her slight build helps.

After we recognize each other, we walk to the train and I notice for the first time the indiscreet looks of men and women following her attractive body and her ambiguous face. They turn to look at us when they hear her powerful, truck driver's voice.

"Do you know anyone in Spain who'd want to marry me?" she asks.

"Let me think . . ."

Vanesa kids around with all the men who glance at her. Every time she sees a somewhat attractive man walk by she says, "There goes my husband." She runs after one, yelling, "Don't go, I'm the woman of your dreams." "Want me to suck you off?" she offers in Spanish. The French men look at her as if she were asking the time.

Back home in Lima, I'd seen officers beating, tear-gassing, and setting their dogs on trans people. I'd read the news coverage on the eviction of "La Pampa de las locas," an area frequented by the poorest trans sex workers. These police raids, named things like

"Prophylaxis 2008," occur despite the fact that sex work isn't a criminal activity in Peru. I'd read in the newspapers that there are organized gangs, such as the now-defunct Los Mojarras, who dedicate themselves to attacking trans people and sex workers.

Every once in a while, a trans person is found brutally murdered under "mysterious circumstances" in their apartment. In 2006, more than five hundred homosexuals were stopped in Peruvian streets across the country, in most cases violently, according to estimates from MHOL (the Movimiento Homosexual de Lima).

Although homosexuality isn't illegal in Peru, marriage between people of the same sex is, and there are no laws that specifically protect the rights of transgender people—a situation that feels a world apart from that of Spain, where the gender identity law was passed in 2007.

In Peru, police are often called to make queer couples leave public spaces for kissing or holding hands. They're escorted out on the basis that "this kind of behavior isn't allowed." A national survey about social exclusion carried out in 2005 by the Peruvian NGO Demus (an organization dedicated to research for the defense of women's rights) showed that in this country riddled with inequality, LGBTQ people were one of the minorities facing most discrimination. Seventy-five percent of Peruvians consider sex between two people of the same gender "wrong," and 30 percent think that homosexuality is a mental disorder.

In this repressive landscape, trans people have formed their own communities. They have even created their own language. They speak *hungarito*, a coded dialect that was born of the need to throw off the police. Words are formed by adding syllables and the letters s and r. For example, *hosorolasara* means *hola*. Try using hungarito to say this prayer, which I once heard a trans person say: "Dear God, make me invisible to the police."

Amelia was told by her gynecologist that hers was a case of ovary hypoplasia, a condition where both ovaries are smaller than normal. She and Melvin wouldn't be able to have children. But their dream to have a child was so fervent, they decided to adopt the daughter of a woman who was going to have an abortion at an illegal clinic. A month after adopting the new-born girl, Amelia discovered that she was pregnant; they left the baby they'd adopted in the care of an aunt and embarked upon this new biological adventure.

They'd been living together for months before they ever made love. They lived with Amelia's mother in her modest home, and the three of them slept in the same bed. One night, her mother couldn't sleep and Amelia moved to the sofa to make her more comfortable. Melvin said he wanted to sleep on the couch with Amelia, and gave her his man's word that nothing would happen. His man's word, of course, was worth nothing. The queer couple had heterosexual sex. Amelia forgot that Melvin was a man with a woman's body. Nine months later, Valery was born.

When she was still a baby, Melvin pretended to nurse her. The little girl started asking for her dad's silicone tit. Amelia would ask Valery to bring her mommy's shoes and she would bring the beaten-up trainers instead of Melvin's golden high heels. If Amelia wore panties, the little girl asked her why she was wearing Daddy's underwear. The boxer shorts were Mommy's. Melvin told Valery that when she grew up those golden heels would be hers. Amelia, meanwhile, took her to all the neighborhood soccer matches.

Valery didn't have two mommies or two daddies. She had a mommy and a daddy. Except everything else was mixed up.

Amelia isn't worried that Valery's dad is a "queen" and her mom is a "butch." Turns out, Valery is a very feminine girl. Amelia suggests sneakers and Valery chooses Barbie shoes.

Sometimes revolutionary parents have reactionary children.

At her first party in Lima after getting her breast implants, Vanesa remembers having seen those *mariconas* arrive in their enormous SUVs—wearing their jewelry and their perfume—and thinking that she wanted to be like them—exactly like one of those trans women who emigrate to Europe and come back to Lima like divas of Italian cinema. Prostitution financed the expensive surgeries that created their powerful female bodies—including sex reassignment operations that cost ten or twelve thousand euros. "How do you do it?" she asked them. One said she did shows, another said she worked in a club, another said she had a millionaire husband. None of them told the truth.

To a Peruvian trans woman, moving to Milan is like being a law student and getting into Harvard. Some leave Peru with fake identities through a well-developed network for illegal immigration that, according to Vanesa, includes people working in the embassy in Lima. All her friends have moved to Milan and, using their earnings from sex work, have built bona fide mansions for their families in the same poor areas on the fringes of Lima where they grew up. In general, they don't move their families to wealthier neighborhoods, opting instead for social signifiers that will stand out in their old barrios: building a second and a third story, installing Jacuzzis, and buying ludicrous cars. Only by sending this kind of money home are they able to ingratiate themselves with their disappointed families.

The filmmaker Felipe de Gregori, director of *Translatina*, a documentary about discrimination against trans people in Peru, believes that migrating allows trans people to make financial contributions to their families, thus earning the respect of their parents, siblings, neighbors, and even society.

"They buy their acceptance with money," says de Gregori, "so their families forget they're trans, they forget that they were once a source of shame for the family, and they start seeing them as benefactors."

In Italy, a trans woman can earn up to three or four hundred euros a day.

"My daughter Georgina thinks money makes you classy, but that's not the way it is." Georgina is another trans woman "who's doing well for herself."

Not only did she build her parents a dream house in Peru, she also had sex reassignment surgery. Vanesa calls Georgina her "daughter" because she was the one who brought Georgina to Paris. "She's got a hundred thousand euros in the bank!" Vanesa bellows.

This system of step-parenting is common among Latin American trans women. Vanesa is Georgina's mother because she covered all her travel costs—around five thousand euros, which is what it costs to get a passport, buy the plane tickets, and get set up in a European city. It works as a loan, more or less. The "daughter" then has to work every night to pay the loan back to her "mother" in cold, hard cash. Being able to pay for a younger trans woman's travel is a symbol of status, and the more daughters Vanesa has, the more prestigious she'll become in the eyes of the older mariconas. Vanesa has two daughters in Paris, and she is also someone else's daughter. She even got her name from her trans mother, Vanesa.

From the start, Vanesa's mother told her there was only one way to get rich in Milan: be a whore. Vanesa the first, however, isn't a whore. She's a thief who's lived in Milan since she was sixteen and is one of the *grandes dames* of the business.

On January 14, 2003, Vanesa left the airport in Lima on a fake passport, dressed as a man, with her hair up. Her tourist visa was valid for fourteen days. The plan was that she'd get to Italy via France, but she never made it to Milan. When she alighted from the metro in the center of Paris, everything seemed so beautiful and welcoming that she thought maybe she wouldn't have to be a whore. She called the other Vanesa in Milan and said she couldn't leave Paris. She said she'd pay off her debt from there, and started cleaning offices.

On one of her first evenings in the City of Light, when she was still staying in a hotel, a Peruvian girl took her to the best club on the Champs-Élysées. An older man came up to her. Alain, he was called; he was a financial adviser in Paris. "The old man," as she calls him, took her home. As Vanesa is telling me this story, I realize that I'm hearing her narrate her own legend. Her six months with Alain—when she could buy Gucci shoes, when she went to Disneyland Paris, when she drove the latest car, and when she brought her two daughters over to Europe—are her lost paradise.

In Peru, she set up a hair salon for one friend and gave another a nose job—that's how she says it, as if she herself had wielded the scalpel. Not only was she able to send money home to Lima, she was also able to visit her friends in Milan. "Work must be good in Paris," they said when they saw her Dior bag.

Vanesa doesn't consider herself a whore: she's a young woman who has "affectionate friends."

"How many women marry for money and never admit it?" she asks.

In her bildungsroman she's the protector of her parents and siblings, and sleeps with old millionaires because she likes them, because she has a soft spot for them.

"My friends said to me: 'Maricón, don't get too hung up on it, just work, make the most of being young.'"

She wasn't going to make it by cleaning office floors, though. That was why she went for old millionaires instead. But what happened? Why did her plans change? She arranges one of her curls over her forehead, and looking at her reflection in the train carriage window says:

"I fell in love and fucked up."

Carmen guessed her brother was gay because clothes kept disappearing from her wardrobe. There was someone else like Melvin in her family, an uncle, so Carmen thought that maybe it was genetic. She was so ashamed that whenever she bumped into Melvin at a party she would rush out in dismay.

One day, Melvin went on a talk show to tell his life story. "If he's doing it to attract attention," his father said, "he should see a psychologist, and if he's doing it for money, he should get a job." When Melvin had his appendix taken out, the doctor told his parents that their son had an excess of female hormones. That was when the disappearances started, and then the ensuing beatings from Dad. Carmen thinks her parents neglected Melvin because of their unhappy marriage. Their dad had gone off with another woman.

Carmen, who sees Valery every now and again, is worried about the girl. Valery talks in slang, has her hair cut boyishly short, just like Amelia, and looks really thin lately. Carmen knows that Amelia's mother, a very elderly woman, is Valery's only caregiver. Amelia goes off to lead her wild life and forgets the girl, says Carmen. When Valery comes to visit, Carmen tries to feed her but Valery won't eat.

"Her stomach has shrunk."

According to Carmen, Valery always asks why her dad wears high heels and lipstick.

She replies that her dad is a clown and that's why he dresses up.

We get off the metro at Quartier Jean-Jaurès, close to Vanesa's apartment on Avenue Secrétan, beside the Gare du Nord and the Canal de l'Ourcq.

"We should go buy some food—I haven't got anything at home."

Vanesa and I walk into the Dia, a run-down Spanish supermarket. Word on the street is that it's bad for your health to buy fruit, vegetables, or meat from there. You have to stick to the tins. Vanesa fills her basket with chips, milk, and Coca-Cola.

All sorts of people live in Vanesa's middle-class neighborhood. "A group of homosexuals hang out beside the canal at night," Vanesa tells me as if she were trying on the role of fussy, gossipy neighbor. She says her apartment is small but has got one big advantage: she doesn't pay anything for it. She rented it providing just her passport for documentation, and one day she stopped paying rent. The landlord eventually took her to court but lost because he'd rented out the apartment to an illegal immigrant.

Having your own place in Paris is no small matter. The first thing I notice about the apartment, really a four-hundred-square-foot room, is its smell. Somehow, improbably and from worlds away, it smells like certain houses in Lima at certain times of day. It's the smell of the evening and of dirty clothes and boiled food and rice and garlic. The heat is always turned all the way up. It's roasting. The cat, Chinchosa, is sleeping on one of the radiators. There's a pair of noisy Australian parakeets. The baroque décor seems to have been sourced from a dumpster. There's an old round table in front of a huge television. A threadbare sofa. A picture of a man in a sled crossing a snowy landscape. A bed at the far side and on the wall some palm leaves bizarrely arranged around a large portrait of Vanesa, as if she were an image of the Virgin. Statuettes of Dalmatians and vases filled with old keys, buttons, one-cent coins. A random assortment of accessories hangs from nails in the wall, such as a feather boa and a Mickey Mouse baseball hat. There are photos of Vanesa posing with other women and a photo of a little girl. The girl, who must be four or five in the photo, is smiling cheekily and making the sign used in Peru to refer to homosexuals: thumb and forefinger making a big ring.

*

I'm intrigued by the improvised tent constructed out of sheets in the middle of the room. Vanesa's husband, Frederic, is asleep inside it. I can't see him; I can only hear his snores and farts.

"*Uy, papi!* Enough sleeping already. Get up."

"We went out last night and got back at six in the morning," she says to me.

I'm starting to feel uncomfortable.

"I met Frederic three days after he got out of prison," Vanesa tells me as she fills the fridge. Frederic, a native Parisian, was busted in Rome with several pounds of cocaine and put away for five years. He was smuggling it in from Brazil. According to Vanesa, Frederic's ex-girlfriend, a Brazilian prostitute, used him as a mule. When he was let out, the first thing he did was call up some prostitutes who happened to be Vanesa's friends. He and Vanesa didn't have sex that night, but they talked until dawn.

"Do you like fried eggs?"

She made me two fried eggs and we ate them with bread and butter and Coca-Cola. A proper Peruvian breakfast.

"That's why I can't marry him, honey, you see? Otherwise I'd have my papers by now. Ha, imagine if we got married. A Peruvian girl married to an ex–drug dealer. They'd pat me down from head to toe in every airport."

She shows me some photos. One is of a blond young man.

"This one wanted to marry me because he thought I was a woman."

When she told him the truth he was devastated.

"He said he thought he'd found the perfect woman to settle down and have kids with. I told him I already have kids. But then he left me."

She shows me a photo of her with Frederic and his family having lunch in the countryside. They look really happy. His family knows she's trans and is supportive. In the photo, Frederic looks tall, muscular, and bald.

"He's a good guy but he's beaten down. There are days when he doesn't bring home a single euro, but I'm not interested in the money."

Frederic was a bus driver until he had an accident. He was driving his car at 125 miles an hour. When they found him, he had his leg behind his head, explains Vanesa, amused. Now he's got metal pins and gets three hundred euros a month in benefits, which doesn't go very far at all.

"But he's clean, he does the laundry, and he can cook a good five-euro meal."

Frederic comes out in boxer shorts and a T-shirt.

"You've slept like a pig, shithead." Soon I realize that swearing constantly is how they show affection. Frederic goes to the kitchen and shouts accusingly:

"Vanesa, what about the chicken?"

"What about it?"

"You haven't boiled it. That takes an hour!"

The man of the house speaks an idiosyncratic mix of French, Italian, and Portuguese. Thanks to our shared Latin root, we can communicate in Spanish.

"I let him sleep in so he wouldn't be in a bad mood, but he's still a pain. Come on, papi, do the cooking and quit whining."

"And have you fed the cat?"

Frederic knows how to swear in perfect Peruvian dialect: *conchatumadre.*

"Yes, she already ate."

The cat is his.

Frederic pours himself a Coca-Cola in silence.

"That man stresses me out, I swear," says Vanesa.

If I'm going to spend the next forty-eight hours with a couple who are either on the brink of a nervous breakdown or of a *lucha libre* match I'd better start finding something to talk about. I ask Frederic for a story I already know: how they met.

"I met Vanesa here in this house when—"

"Shut up, I already told her."

"You're not the most affectionate, are you, Vanesa?" I say, unable to stop myself.

"I'm very affectionate," says Frederic in Spanish, "but he's not."

I remembered that in French "she" (*elle*) is pronounced like the Spanish "he" (*él*).

When Vanesa looked like a man and was called Melvin, she worked collecting fares on buses. One day, Melvin's father asked why she was obsessed with dressing like a woman. It was fine to be gay, but there was no reason to draw attention to oneself. His father had friends at the bank who were gay and lived one life at home and another in public. To please him, Melvin cut her hair short, crying. After she dropped out of a degree course in Hospitality and Tourism at San Martín University to become a woman, her father stopped talking to her.

Sometimes, reactionary parents have revolutionary children.

My head is pounding and I think I'm getting a fever. I have to go into the bathroom as soon as possible and use the breast pump to empty myself out or I run the risk of getting an infection. I milk myself over Vanesa's bathtub using my hands, because I can't get the pump to work. Right now, I'd give anything for a pair of silicone tits, anything to be free from my female condition. I wonder if this antagonism is akin to how trans people feel about their own bodies. Vanesa, meanwhile, is changing her top. She leaves her almost perfect tits on show and I can't avoid comparing them to mine. The curiosity is killing me, and I ask if I can touch them.

"Of course!"

"They don't feel weird . . . "

"They're normal, see? You can even push them together."

"They're pretty soft, they seem natural . . . "

"Yeah, I was lucky."

"They never get old. They're better than real ones . . . "

"They usually sag."

"Ah, so fake ones sag too . . . "

"I've got a friend who looks like she's breastfed five puppies, six kittens, and four piglets. But somehow mine haven't sagged. People say they can burst, but these have been through fistfights . . . and nothing."

Vanesa's operations: nose, saline serum prosthetic breasts—the good thing about saline or serum is that if the prosthesis ever bursts, the body absorbs it, she explains—and lots of hormones. Also, silicone that she injected in her hips herself because the operation was too expensive. She bought some needles at the pharmacy and shut herself in a room in a hostel. She filled every corner of her masculine body with fatty liquid and immediately softened into feminine roundness. Her tits, on the other hand, were done by a Peruvian surgeon for twelve hundred dollars.

"I didn't finish paying for them. I only gave him seven hundred dollars. He told me to bring the rest when I went back to have the stitches out. I never went back. I just took the stitches out with nail clippers."

Vanesa really likes herself. She's almost unbearably vain. She talks about her body and congratulates herself on her good fortune constantly. Her body looks like a twenty-something woman's. Thanks to her bone structure, she's delicate rather than crudely curvy.

Vanesa isn't considering sex reassignment surgery.

"One friend had the tip of her penis surgically altered to form a clitoris. She says she feels like she's coming but doesn't ejaculate. And I've got another friend who says she can't feel a thing, not even when she pees. She tells her husband 'put it inside me,' and he goes 'I already did.' I'll always be a man. I can't fake being a woman even if I get the operation. I'm already going against God as I am, imagine if I got the op. I'd like to have been born a woman but it wasn't to be."

We go out for a walk around the neighborhood, and as we watch all sorts of men pass us by she tells me the truth:

"I haven't had the surgery because if I do, I'm out of business. I'll have it done when I can't get it up anymore."

In the photograph, Amelia is about six years old. Her mom dressed her up in a white dress and braided her long hair. It's her baptism.

At age eleven, she refused to wear anything other than a tracksuit to school. When her mother asked her where her uniform skirt was, she always said it was dirty.

Eventually, she had to accept that her daughter was a tomboy—a *chito*. What had she done wrong?

Amelia liked being with men to understand how they dressed and how they spoke; to imitate them. She could only fall in love with girls. Until she met Vanesa.

When I mention Amelia in front of Frederic, he says: "Oh! Michael, Vanesa's wife." They haven't heard from her in more than a month. According to Vanesa, Amelia has been getting drunk on the money she was sending her. She tells me they'll always be a family, but that she's pretty fed up with Amelia.

"It's not like I'm sexist, but if I protect her I expect her to appreciate it. I asked her not to let me down and she did."

When they separated, Vanesa told her that she would always support her.

"Now she's gone off with a prostitute. She called me and told me. I just told her to look after herself."

"Maybe she was getting drunk because she missed you . . . "

"Do you know how much money I spent calling her? Eight hundred euros, which my old man paid for. I would play songs for her and we'd cry all night."

Tonight, Frederic and Vanesa will take me to the woods. Le Bois de Boulogne is a park on the western edge of Paris, close to the suburb of Boulogne-Billancourt. According to Wikipedia, it's more than twice as large as Central Park and much larger than London's Hyde Park. During the Hundred Years' War, outlaws would hide in the woods. Henry IV planted fifteen thousand mulberry trees in the hope of establishing a local silk industry. His disowned wife, Marguerite de Valois, took refuge there. The area was turned into a park by Napoleon III in 1852. Parisians called it "The Garden of Earthly Pleasures," but, like El Bosco's painting, it's no paradise. Robert Bresson's *The Ladies of the Bois de Boulogne* tells the story of a woman who was forced to work as a prostitute in these woods. Le Bois once housed around fifteen hundred sex workers, but a few years ago it was "cleaned out," and now only a few women and several hundred trans people remain, mostly undocumented Latin American immigrants.

I feel really feverish and definitely have an infection. My breasts are as hard as rocks. Vanesa is sleeping. After eating the chicken stew Frederic made, we've been resting at home. I've been going into the bathroom every hour to drain some milk, but it isn't enough. I need to go to a hospital to get an electric breast pump that can relieve the pain I'm in. Vanesa refuses to go with me; she acts like a temperamental and inconsiderate child when anyone tries to get her out of bed. I tell them I'm going to the hospital alone, but Frederic offers to go with me. We head for the maternity ward, which turns out not to have a damned breast pump. They advise me to keep squeezing it out by hand. When we get back to the apartment, Vanesa tells me sleepily that the same thing happened to Michael when she was nursing Valery. She teaches me how to squeeze the milk out properly.

Although she hasn't told me this explicitly, Vanesa works as a prostitute. At first, she tries to convince me that she's only going to the woods this one night to earn a few extra euros. Eventually she'll tell me she has an ad with her phone number on a website, but that it doesn't bring her much work. When clients come to her place, she charges them up to fifty euros to have sex in the bed where, she tells me, I'm going to sleep tonight. But it's simpler to go to the woods, where she earns thirty euros per client but the flow is steady and sometimes the clients are more generous.

"I did kids' theater and I danced in cabarets. I wanted to prove that trans people from Latin America don't come here just to walk the streets, but eventually I had no choice."

Frederic tells me that French men aren't judgmental, that when they love someone it doesn't matter whether their lover is a man or a whore or both. Before handing her over to all the city's degenerates, he runs his girlfriend a lovely bubble bath that she sourly rejects.

"I've told you a thousand times not to put bubbles in it!"

"You think I'm your slave?"

"Oooh, look how macho you are!"

It's the first time I've been out whoring with a whore. Vanesa puts on skinny jeans and a top. It's incredibly cold in Paris tonight and in the woods, they tell me, it's even worse. Vanesa isn't wearing a coat.

"I'd rather freeze than starve."

We get into Frederic's beat-up car. Vanesa's husband knows the world of prostitution like the back of his hand. Two of his ex-partners were prostitutes. He tells me that for a while he'd been working as a driver for the trans prostitutes, but that he's unemployed just now. He would pick them up at home and charge ten euros to take them to the edge of the woods.

Frederic speeds the whole way and runs all the red lights.

"Wasn't Lady Di killed around here?" I joke, but their only reply is that she died somewhere else.

I can imagine the headlines: "Drug dealer, trans woman, and journalist die in car crash on the way to the whoring woods."

"People who go to the woods want to know what you've got between your legs."

Vanesa, who really should be featured in an anthology of Latin American dirty realism, can jolt you out of anything—even my bourgeois anxiety over death.

"Some people think you're a woman but when they find out you're not they don't care. They're often really into it. They tell me it's their first time and ask me if they can touch me. Before you know it, they're down on their knees acting out their repressed fantasies. Everyone's got their own drama."

Vanesa can be vulgar but dreams of being treated like a sensitive girl. Everyone's got their own drama.

Michael knew Vanesa had fallen in love with someone else and was thinking of staying in Paris. At first Michael felt lonely and looked for another partner. Now he lives with a different woman and with little Valery. He says he's really in love with this woman. Sometimes Valery looks at photos of Vanesa and says: "My daddy's really pretty." Michael has told Valery that his new partner is his best friend. They all go out together, with her kids, too, who Valery calls her brothers and sisters.

According to Michael, Vanesa hasn't sent any money for her daughter in more than a year. And even when she did send money, it happened very sporadically. He knows she's had problems but he really needs the money. He works as a bag boy, sometimes through the night. If he gets home before eight he takes his daughter to school in the mornings. Melvin ended up with a guy and Amelia with a girl.

*

The woods appear before my eyes, cut in two by the road we're speeding along on. On both sides it looks dark, shadowy, and deep. The vision lends itself to all sorts of *Lord of the Rings*–styled sexual fantasies full of wigs, fur coats, and gold boots—although these characters aren't exactly elves.

Once, a guy asked Vanesa to tie him up and then the police appeared so she ran off and left him there.

Vanesa enjoys demolishing stereotypes: she tells me that Arabs often insult her, but then beg for her to penetrate them. She tells me there's lots of black men with small dicks. And plenty of Algerian trans people.

Frederic drops us off at the place where the Peruvian girls gather. There we find two compatriots taking a break from work. They're eating Chinese takeout they've just bought from an Ecuadorian, same as every night. One of them is Vanesa's other European daughter, Tatiana. They're talking about a hairdresser who used to be a nursery school teacher. Tatiana let the hairdresser stay at her house a couple of days, and she supposedly hit on her husband, who, of course, she'd met in the woods. "The new girls always want to snatch up what it's taken us years of work to get," says Betina, the eldest in the group. Her disillusionment sharply contrasts the enthusiasm of the young Brazilian who's shouting in a frenzy: "I'm a woman, I'm a woman!"

"They always take her for a maricona," explains Vanesa.

The small Brazilian girl opens her coat to the wind and braves the cold to show the traffic her naked breasts and tiny thong. The lights illuminate her and for a moment she's the figure on the prow of a ship. She lowers her thong, pushes apart the jungle of hair, and proudly shows us she's a real woman. She runs a finger along herself and licks it as if she were in a porn film. She's surely under the effect of some magnificent drug. Some girls in the woods take drugs to withstand the cold and the hours of hard work.

"Vanesa has got a nice body, and because she's small, she can pass for a woman. But the Brazilian acts like a transvestite. You don't need to be a woman to be feminine." Betina is scathing. "And the Brazilian is a nymphomaniac," adds Tatiana.

I watch Vanesa, with all her manufactured femininity, walk off toward the cars that are lining up to see her. If she stayed with us she wouldn't be able to work. Especially because Frederic, sporting an intimidating pimp demeanor, has just returned.

Just then an old Peugeot pulls up next to us. There's a woman inside. It's Frederic's sister, who's temporarily inherited the underground taxi service. Frederic invites me on a tour of the woods while we wait for Vanesa to do her thing. I ride shotgun beside his sister, a big woman called Florence who's wearing glasses and an alpaca poncho, a gift from one of the Peruvian girls. Florence was depressed and weighed two hundred and sixty pounds, Frederic informs me. Now she's lost nearly a third of her weight and is trying to turn things around for herself.

Frederic is friendly with all the women. He says hi from the car window and tells me who's who. We stop beside a very tall dark-skinned woman who is shivering at the side of the road, and Frederic says to her, "Hola, Carolina, say hi to your husband from me." This is a microcosm of Latin America. That woman's Argentinian. This one's Peruvian but has Spanish papers. That one there is Ñata. She makes delicious ceviche. That's the Ecuadorian who sells the girls food. And this woman here is Paloma; she used to be a police officer in Peru. That's Shirley, another Peruvian. She went to college and is really smart. Fifteen to twenty people in Ecuador could live off what that girl standing there does with her ass every night. And this one coming over now has AIDS, so the French government gives her food, accommodation, medication, and even papers.

According to the Paris organization PASTT (Prevention, Action, Health, Work for Transgender People), which works with the girls in the woods, there are hundreds of ongoing applications for residents' permits, accommodation, and legal assistance with immigration papers, because most trans people in here are foreigners. None of their applications ever gets a reply.

At only 5'2" and with my moderate proportions, I feel invisible among all these statuesque women. I wonder what a world without cisgender women would be like. Trans women sometimes seem the projection of what men think women should be, which is why heterosexual men like trans women so much. In these times, they're the closest they'll get to their feminine ideal.

Florence has to leave us. Frederic and I wander around in search of Vanesa, who we haven't seen for more than an hour.

"It's a bit of a strange life, don't you think?" Frederic says. "And by strange I mean shitty." I look at him and realize Frederic is a sensitive person.

It's below zero and I'm running a high fever. Frederic walks much like he drives. He makes me cross the street on a red light at a dangerous junction. My breasts still feel as though they're ready to explode.

Not long ago, the police arrested Vanesa in the woods because she's—what? trans? a sex worker? an illegal immigrant? To be let out, she had to tell them she was Cuban and that in her country queer people get killed. When she got out of custody she called her family in Peru seeking comfort, but all they wanted to know was when she'd send money. So she changed her number. That was why it was difficult for me to track her down.

Gone are the golden days when she was the angel in drag looking out for her maricona sisters. Now she's in love with her good-natured, white trash, intelligent pimp, who treats her like a spoiled child and runs her bubble baths.

Vanesa emerges from the woods looking like a bruised pixie. She's made ninety euros in an hour, but she's in a foul mood because she just dropped a ten and can't find it.

Before we get home, we stop at a shop, and with tonight's money we buy bread, ham, cheese, butter, cookies, and chocolate. They want to treat me. When we get home, we bundle up in their den with the heating turned up to the max and eat together, feeling nearly cheerful. Then I remember that Frederic's children are far away tonight, as are Vanesa's. He told me this a few hours ago on the way to the maternity ward. Their mother took them to Brazil and he hasn't seen them since. We're all far away from our children. I wonder if they think about them. I let a bit more milk run down the plughole while I take a bubble bath. According to the girls in the woods, taking a bath helps them feel better when they get home after a night of work. In the bed where Vanesa sometimes makes her living, I fall asleep on my coat.

#NOTPEE

MARIANA'S EX-BOYFRIEND was expecting me at five p.m. in his apartment in the center of Barcelona. I'm a few minutes early. I get out of the taxi and dial his number. "Hi, it's Gabriela." "Come on up," says the voice. I hesitate, glance back, think about making a run for it, but I don't. In the elevator, I pray that everything is clean, that it's not too unpleasant, that he doesn't rape me, that he doesn't kill me. I tell myself I'm crazy for doing this, that I've either got massive balls or a tiny brain. I'm regretting this, but it's too late now; he's already opening the door. Last night, sometime after my fourth drink, I told people at the bar I was writing a piece about female ejaculation, but that I'd come to a dead end because I hadn't been able to meet with the elusive Ninja Squirt, the guy who became popular for masturbating women while dressed as a ninja. He'd become a sex therapist of sorts and was now charging two hundred euros per training session. In an email he'd sent me from Thailand, he said if I was after an article he wasn't interested, but if I wanted to embark on "a path of self-discovery" we could talk. His mission, he wrote, consisted of "connecting women with their deepest sexuality" by helping us "activate the pulsations of the womb, the center of power, to achieve empowerment that transcends the realm of sexuality."

I didn't have a cent and, try as I might, no newspaper would pay for me to reach my center of power. I'd been left wavering between disappointment and one more drink that night at the bar, until Mariana called me to one side and resuscitated my floundering article. She raved about her ex, calling him a "genital Spider-Man."

"What?"

"Yeah, 'Spider-Man' is the technique that makes you squirt. He puts his fingers inside you as if he were going to spray spiderwebs between buildings."

She told me he'd done it to her plenty of times, and that he was even well-known for it beyond Barcelona's sexual underground. "He's fast and lethal," she added. I asked her if she'd be willing to go with me, but they'd broken up so recently that she couldn't imagine anything more awkward. The things we do for journalism, Mariana concluded, and called him. "He says yes, but he has to get back to work at seven."

Why do I have to get a guy to do it for me? Is female ejaculation the business of men, ninjas, professionals, experts with long fingers and strong, muscular arms? Why not try doing it myself? The part of me that likes being in control of things, orgasms included, feels disgusting as I knock on his door, but I do so anyway. I need to find out if it's real. I need to squirt. He invites me into the bedroom. He's a weird guy, but thankfully more odd than psychopathic. He invites me to sit on the bed and he sits in a chair. The conversation is brief and technical. We discuss how it might be hard for me to get turned on. He tells me to take everything off from the waist down and lie on the bed. "Do you want to touch yourself or should I do it?"

"You do it," I say. I'm drier than the Atacama Desert.

*

I've wound up on a stranger's bed because I can't squirt. I want to soak beds with my floodgates. I want to turn into the Trevi Fountain when I fuck and shower my lovers' faces. I want there to be a splash zone to my orgasms. The almost biblical mystery of female ejaculation seems to me the black hole of women's sexuality. Can we all ejaculate? Is it a matter of physiology or one of training? Maybe I was fixating on what my friend MF once told me: "I come and it's lovely, but squirting is like the pot of gold at the end of the rainbow. The fucking rainbow. The aurora borealis. You laugh like an idiot and if you were to go out into the streets afterward the universe would probably send a car to run you over just because you're so insufferably radiant." But it had only happened to her once in her forty years. "It's the kind of thing that's best when it's rare." Yeah, right.

I'd already been wondering if there was such a thing as the Great Orgasm, a kind of orgasm that would combine squirting and coming, when I talked to Elena, a journalist, friend, and squirting activist. She explained that she could achieve El Dorado with clitoral masturbation and the right pressure on her G-spot. Elena says sometimes she ejaculates and doesn't come, and other times she comes but doesn't ejaculate. And sometimes she does both together. Orgasm and ejaculation are different things, but, as Elena confirmed, they can happen simultaneously. Soon after our talk I got to see Elena come while ejaculating, and I couldn't hide my envy. It was worse than if she'd published a better book than mine.

Which didn't prevent me from supporting those who took affront at the ban in the UK and the recent scientific finding—or rather the clumsy insult—that concluded that female ejaculation is nothing but pee. The trending hashtag #notpee and photos of damp sheets and puddles on floors and carpets from female ejaculators everywhere in response to the UK's ban on squirting in pornography fed my curiosity. When I ask another of my friends if she squirts, she replies: "I'm happy if I come at all. And now on top of that I'm supposed to worry about ejaculating?" Hers seems like a healthy approach, but I'm neither healthy nor easily satisfied. I have a tendency to ruminate, to lean in toward that voice that whispers: "What if I'm an incomplete woman?" It's like being an only child: you can live without the siblings you never had, but you'll always wonder if you missed out.

And now I'm here. I feel like a broken machine that has to be hammered back into working order. This is a waste of time, I tell myself. The feeling is pretty unpleasant. "If you feel like you're going to pee, don't hold it in," he says. By this point I'm on the floor on all fours. I notice that there's hard rock playing in the background. The perfect soundtrack for this hard, deep onslaught. He whispers to me attentively: "I've got the mop ready." I can almost hear the grinding teeth of my vagina dentata.

I've always been suspicious of the fact that only in the genre of squirting porn does the authenticity of female orgasms go unquestioned. I've rolled my eyes at Cytherea, the queen of jet-wash pornography, and scorned all those gurus of ejaculation who profit off of promises that we'll only "free our real selves" if we squirt. As if pleasure had to be visible to be real. As if orgasms could be measured or compared. As if sex were about spectacle and not intimacy.

I piss myself. I feel something very strange approaching. Something desperate, unbearable, that starts and stops. And yes, this must be it. I can see the water emerging from between my legs, transparent, clean, and falling to the floor, just within reach of the mop. "It wasn't easy; for a moment I thought you wouldn't get there," he says.

But I haven't come. What good is squirting if I don't come? I'm sure there's a pop song in that.

While his fingers are making their slippery getaway, I think that one of these days, with everything I've learned, I might achieve the perfect orgasm, electric and aquatic. Maybe it doesn't exist, or maybe it's already happened. Maybe I'll just carry on with my unexotic orgasms, getting wet and then coming. I stand up, and before my masturbator can mop it up, I run my finger through the puddle. I smell it, I taste it. It's not pee.

THE GREATER THE BEAUTY,
THE MORE IT IS BEFOULED

SERGEI PANKEJEFF IS CRYING in front of his doctor. His nose
swells and turns violently red with the spasms of his sobs. It's very
simple: in his dream, there was a heap of white wolves, completely
still, staring at him from the tree outside his window. Sigmund
Freud strokes his beard while Pankejeff sobs. Today, he's not interested in analyzing the vision of his father savagely penetrating
his mother, the time his sister pulled down her underwear and
told him to "eat this," or all the things he dreamed of doing to his
English schoolmistress before she caught him looking at her and
threatened to cut off a piece of his penis. All Sergei wants is for
the still white wolves that are perched dove-like on the branches to
disappear, but the white wolves, immutable, continue their vigil.

A few years after finishing psychoanalysis with Freud, the
white wolves gave way to yet another psychotic delirium: Pankejeff
began to obsessively stare at his reflection, convinced that
someone had drilled a hole in his nose. Mirrors determinedly
announced that he was a damned Cindy Sherman photograph,
that his face was a trypophobic's nightmare, and that his nose,
especially his nose, was a turd. Poor rich Russian.

I suffer from body dysmorphia disorder, the same condition
Pankejeff was afflicted with and that psychoanalysts attempted,
in vain, to cure. Like the Russian aristocrat, I worry obsessively

about things I consider to be defects in my physical appearance. The most disturbing thing about a condition like this is that the defect in question may be real or imaginary. I feel like I should be classified alongside two-headed turtles, babies born with their twins inside them, and cats with six legs, but whether my defects are fact or fiction is unclear.

No one can quite put me down like I can. That is my victory. I'm constantly tallying my grotesque attributes: crooked teeth; dark knees; fat arms; sagging breasts; little eyes engulfed in two big, black bags; greasy, spotty nose; witch-like hair; incipient humpback; double chin; scars; hairy, bulging armpits; blotchy skin covered in freckles and moles; small, dark hands; jagged nails; lack of waist and curves; flat ass; ten pounds too many; bristly pubic hair; anal hair; big, brown nipples; stretched and drooping stomach; voice; breath; the smell of my vagina—my fetidness. And I've still got old age ahead of me. And decomposition.

There was a time when I used to make collages with cut-out photos of myself. I'd join parts of my imperfect body with clippings of models' incredible bodies. In one of my self-portraits, I have a ruby on my nipple and the body of an erotic comic book heroine from the seventies.

Nietzsche put it like this: "man mirrors himself in things; he considers everything beautiful that reflects his own image. . . . Ugliness is understood as a sign and a symptom of degeneration." People generally take for granted that there are ugly people in the world, but they never imagine themselves in that category. No one wants to be merely pleasant. There are few things as obsolete as inner beauty. On occasion, I've applied myself to the task of meticulously judging others aesthetically. We all know that this exercise has no allure for beautiful people. Genuinely good-looking people don't even realize how good-looking they are. For ugly people, this isn't merely a topic of conversation; it's an all-consuming occupation. In fact, it's safe to say that anyone who isn't interested in talking about other people's bodies must be somewhat good-looking. Conversely, an average or even fairly attractive person is made significantly uglier by talking about the beauty of others.

If my lovers or friends are ugly, I think they make me uglier by association. The same goes for what I write. What I write always makes me uglier. I won't go into my hatred for good writers who are also marvelously hot. I've got several of them buried in my backyard. Beauty kills, no? For Bataille, "beauty is desired in order that it may be befouled; not for its own sake, but for the joy brought by the certainty of profaning it. . . . The greater the beauty, the more it is befouled."

I think very few people are attracted to me at first sight. So few, that I'm always surprised when it happens. Of course, some people find me attractive when they get to know me. They might see my large breasts, my shiny black hair, and my small, defined mouth, which gives me a touch of exoticism and helplessness. When I'm naked I look like a recently captured Amazonian tribe-woman, and that turns people on, turns their inner colonizer on—or so I'm told by my lovers and friends.

In his essay "On Ugliness," Umberto Eco, an unquestionably ugly man, cites Marcus Aurelius—notably nicknamed "the wise" and not "the handsome"—to validate the beauty of what is imperfect, the beauty of "cracks in a loaf of bread." Argentinian poet Alejandra Pizarnik, who committed suicide at the age of thirty-six, also thought herself ugly. In one of her poems, she wrote: "You wish you were another. The other one you are wishes she were another." This is the phrase I chose for my Facebook tagline. Never have a few words taken out of context defined me better.

Loving a beautiful man and being loved by one isn't exclusively the birthright of beautiful women. In Ettore Scola's film *Passion of Love*, a handsome Italian soldier meets Lady Fosca. Sickly, hysterical, with her bony, anemic face, her mouse ears, and her long nose, Fosca falls in love with the handsome young man. Beauty and the beast in reverse.

There is nothing ugly women desire more than beauty. Fosca's narcissism is a thirst that can never be quenched. Her inner world is shadowy, her desire is unrequited. And she chases him. She humiliates herself for him, she gives herself over desperately and savagely, her longing elevates her, even beautifies her. Hers is a subversive love; some cretins might call it suicidal. Fosca doesn't truly love the man; she loves the man's beauty and dreams of possessing it. His beauty is the mirror in which she sees herself, and her ugliness is the mirror for his morality. The spiderwebs she spins ensnares this pious and deeply flattered man. So the handsome captain helps her, accompanies her, cares for her, embraces Fosca with his gaze, and gives her the affection and attention the world has denied her. He is transformed from a state of mere beauty to one of tragic magnanimity.

In the photo posted on an anonymous blog, I was sitting on the ground eating a banana. The photo is followed by 395 comments in which people—men, predominantly—accuse me of being a slut and of "letting myself go" now that I'm married. Being called a slut is not something that's ever particularly upset me, so let's not waste time on that. But that other thing, that self-evident truth . . .

If body dysmorphia is a mental illness, am I imagining it all? Am I in fact beautiful? If I'm fabricating my unattractiveness, why are so many people writing about it? Why does a beautiful man love me? Should I be beautiful? Does my ugliness justify their pain, their appetite, their virulence? Is their aggression more about my moral than my physical impurity? Is it a combination of both? Am I crazy to ask myself these questions? Does no one else ask themselves these things? Despite my disorder, or maybe precisely because of it, someone who loves me once said: "I wish I'd met you when you were little, so that I could have told you that you were the most beautiful girl in the world." In the drawing I made based on this phrase, he travels to the past, finds me, sits me on his knee, tells me I'm beautiful—and I believe him. In this alternative story of my life, I grow up without the disorder and never tally my flaws.

THREE

I NEVER GOT THE KNACK OF FIDELITY. Ever since I first experienced pleasure outside the four walls of the most sacred pacts of love, I've continually enjoyed transgressive sex. At first, I put this preference down to my lack of cohesion and inability to assert my desires. How could I enjoy unfaithfulness without sacrificing Sunday movie nights and breakfasts in bed? How could I savor the excitement of a secret rendezvous but still cuddle with someone who loved and protected me? For years a wicked, ancient voice has whispered to me: "You can't have it all. You have to choose." But I've never been able to choose. I wanted it all, and I decided to subvert love, that imperfect model, the deadly trap that had hopelessly condemned me to the miseries of a double life. So I started a guerrilla war. If the groundwork wasn't yet laid for a true revolution, I figured I might at least start crusading by participating in clandestine meetings with lovers, writing them coded letters, and perpetrating attacks against reactionary targets—i.e., my partners. I was an avenger battling for sexual freedom. I went out at night, wearing my mask and patched-up latex suit, to place small charges of dynamite against the wall of monogamy.

I've been unfaithful to everyone I've ever dated. I've been unfaithful in a stairway, on several buses, in dozens of zero-star hotels, under a starry sky, on a beach, in a parking lot, in a museum, right under their noses. I've been unfaithful on Good Friday, Mother's Day, Christmas, and even during a coup d'état. Drunk, sober, first thing in the morning, and last thing at night. I've been unfaithful with my neighbors, my classmates, my workmates, my exes, my male friends, my female friends, their best friends, their other selves, enticing strangers, and less than enticing strangers, as forgettable as they are numerous. With six people the same day, two the same night, three in the same bed. I've been unfaithful to my lovers. And, of course, I ended up marrying one of them.

Jaime is a poet and, although he tries desperately hard to act like a rational being, tends to behave like a superhero whose powers have been usurped by an unknown villain. He's inward-looking, impenetrable, you never know what he's really thinking; you could say he's a great big bag of complexes but, and I'm in no doubt about this, there's not a selfish bone in him. He's noble and true. We both, more or less, share an idea of what a man should be. I suppose that's why we're together.

I met Jaime when I was stuck in a dying relationship, and he became my lover. For him, I was nothing more than an occasional fling: he never showed any romantic interest in me until I broke up with his rival once and for all. Jaime was innocent. I was the one who'd decided to lie, I was the one doing the cheating. Or at least that's what he wanted to believe. Jaime saw himself as nothing more than a spare part in my story, and felt pretty comfortable as such. But then something unexpected happened: we fell in love.

One of my favorite authors, Philip Roth, wrote: "If you don't go crazy because of your husband's vices, you go crazy because of his virtues." A year into our relationship, Jaime and I were living together. We were very different, but we'd decided to throw ourselves wholeheartedly into our new family setup. I thought this meant the end of an era and my initiation into the paradise of monogamy, which thus far had proved incomprehensible and elusive. Jaime loved it. It hadn't taken long for him to go from cynical lover to protective companion. It was like watching an award ceremony where an actor swears he'd been waiting all his life to play the exact role he's being lauded for. But our differences soon became clear. Jaime was repulsed by my fantasies, my excesses, the whole framework around which I'd built my sexual identity up to then. He couldn't stand the thought of anyone else invading our bed, not even as a hypothetical to indulge my fantasies. It's not like I was free from jealousy myself. In fact, the mere thought of Jaime falling for another woman or feeling emotionally attached to someone else filled me with anxiety. But in Jaime's case those feelings revolved almost exclusively around sex. What's more, his jealousy was like most men's: retroactive, something I'll never understand. For me, asking Jaime (read: forcing Jaime) to tell me the details of his sexual encounters was a way for me to appropriate them. Why did he find it so painful to even imagine me with somebody else? When it came to my past, Jaime felt like the biblical Lot: if he looked back, he ran the risk of turning into a pillar of salt.

I once read in an encyclopedia that a jealous man has far more powerful orgasms and ejaculates more sperm than a man who feels confident in the love promised to him. (So, really, my exes ought to be thanking me for those potent orgasms, their sperm like little Star Wars soldiers ready to tear their intergalactic competition to shreds.) Jealousy is not just a desire for absolute possession or an ego problem. I don't believe there's an intrinsic conservation mechanism driven by the "wisdom of the species," like that cretin Schopenhauer said, either. Jealousy is clearly an irrational, instinctive reaction, an indestructible bunker of a social construct we've built to encase ourselves.

Jaime and I were barely surviving the stifling incarceration of monogamy until, unexpectedly, things changed. I don't know exactly when the idea of having a threesome went from being a bedroom joke to a family project; maybe two became too lonely a number. The suggestion to have a threesome is one of the many dubious and self-serving projects I've introduced to our relationship. By the time I'd met Jaime, I'd already stomached the bittersweet experience of seeing my partner with another woman. It's initially as unpleasant as using a stranger's toothbrush. Watching someone you love have sex with someone else is a feeling that concentrates around your middle, one of those painful experiences you know will do you good sooner or later.

I've always been a firm believer in not having limits, especially when it comes to sex. I don't remember how I started taking part in threesomes and later suggesting them; they weren't in fashion yet, there weren't television programs or films about threesomes or famous people talking about their multitudinous love lives. I was sixteen years old. I was sleeping with a guy who was older than me. He was the one who first showed me a porn film in which two blond women moved their tongues up and down the same cock. Grateful for this pedagogical overture, I tried to impress him with my schoolgirl stories. I liked telling him about my masturbatory rituals in the bathroom at home. It made me feel powerful to describe the celibate games I had played with my girlfriends, especially when it had been my turn to be the dominating one. As far as I can remember, there was nothing more exciting at the age of ten than having a friend stay over and playing at touching each other in the dark, in silence, almost accidentally. Many of my adult perversions likely harken back to those fairy story kisses under the covers.

I'm not sure if it was about his desire or mine, but in any case, my first boyfriend and I let one of my friends into our bed. Or rather, we got into hers—her parents' bed, to be precise. We didn't have a big enough bed yet and weren't old enough for hotels. That morning I watched aghast as someone else rode the man I considered my property, my inalienable right—and something inside me shattered forever. At the moment of tripartite lovemaking, jealousy and desire competed with equal ferocity, and the pleasure of exclusivity was replaced by the pleasure of being one among many. I'm not sure if what I'm saying is quite true, though, because after all I was the official girlfriend, a Countess Báthory overseeing the sacrifice of virgins. I learned that, whenever possible, it's best to avoid being the third person. From my bureaucratic fiefdom, I decided who I shared my boyfriend with, for how long, and to what degree. That was my prerogative.

After my first threesome with another woman, I demanded one with two men. I took it very seriously. My boyfriend owed it to me. We started looking and one night, when we were both very drunk, we found two guys who seemed nice. They followed us to the beach without a word. That night I did it with the two of them while my boyfriend closely supervised the action.

Once you've got the hang of threesomes, you start to feel like the gonzo director of a porn film, continually trying to make the cast hotter and more skilled. As a threesome aesthete, I didn't want my attempts to stage *Jules et Jim* to end up looking like the Three Little Pigs, and for a while, I devoted most of my late adolescence to finding the perfect formula. If sex is a question of numerology, then three has surely proven to be my lucky number. Three is speculative, it evokes the cosmos and the infinite.

As my relationship with Jaime progressed, I felt an increasing desire to reproduce the explosive, tenuous experiences I'd had as a teenager. I had to press the issue, but not much. Once the details had been ironed out (in other words, when I'd promised we'd only do it with other women), we set to work. I know it doesn't look like a fair deal from the outside, but I was emerging from an impressive era of cheating that I intended to purge by allowing my new love glamorous freedom, albeit within limits I would set. What's more, I, like so many other women, like women. Sometimes, I like to reunite with my own substance, I like to feel in another woman what a man feels in me. When a woman kisses me on the lips, I'm aroused by the softness, smoothness, and suppleness that I intuit in my own body.

To cut a long story short, Jaime and I eventually did find someone. She was a friend of mine, one of those friends who's always been there. She wasn't a very sociable person; in fact, she was fairly manic and permanently sarcastic. I knew her well, but was still caught off guard by her strange spells of aggression. She was no Anaïs Nin, but neither were we Henry and June. That winter we started seeing a lot of each other. We met up every afternoon and talked about sex.

The first triple kiss happened in a terrible bar in the center of Lima. First, she told Jaime to kiss her. He glanced at me first and I nodded. Then he kissed her, then me, then her, then I kissed her, then we both kissed him. A triple kiss is something strange. Three mouths come together like three chicks fighting for the same worm.

The threat of death hovers over any threesome constantly. Take, for example, Jaime driving twenty over the speed limit while she and I lavish damp caresses on each other in the back seat. We're naked and kissing so hard we bite each other. She comes on Calle X. Me, on the corner of Calle Y. This is a scene from real life, it happened that same night as that first triple kiss, but it could also work metaphorically. Simultaneity is the utopia of a threesome. She might be driving while Jaime and I roll around in the back. Or it might be me driving while they stain the upholstery and steam up the windows. In that case, wanting to get home and join in, I'd accelerate until the car got smashed to bits.

The outcome of a threesome is as hazardous as any car accident. Our own three-way collision resulted in one casualty.

First came the abortion. She knew what she had to do and that morning we went with her to the clinic. To keep her from feeling sad we stupidly played with the idea of having it, a child with Jaime's nose, her Asian eyes, and my overconfident personality.

We'd live under the same roof and read Harry Potter together. I experienced the despair of an abortion from the other side, the waiting room, that day. When it was all over we went out for dinner and drank a lot of wine.

One night in our gorgeous triple bed, she started crying inconsolably while we made love as only three people can. Jaime was behind her so that when he rocked up and down the echoes of their shared movements reached my pubis. Finally, Jaime lowered himself onto me. And that was when she started crying. We hugged her, but it was no use. I think by then we'd talked too much. It was as if all the damage we'd caused her had been hidden just beneath her skin and suddenly came to the surface before our eyes.

"I want to go," she said.

Jaime took her home. It was an especially cold night. I stayed in bed, feeling grateful that, for once, I wasn't the one going to shit. I felt like I do whenever I see a couple fighting in public: relieved I'm not them. I was grateful that we were three and not two. That I wasn't the girlfriend in distress and that there was someone else who could deal with it.

When they arrived at her building, she didn't move to get out of the car.

"You bastard!" she shouted at Jaime while trying to hit him.

And Jaime, the politest, sweetest person I know, pushed her out of the car and drove home.

When she left for good, our bed felt huge, unimaginably huge. That was when we decided to explore the incredibly limited market of prostitutes for couples.

*

In a threesome, there are always two exhibitionists and a voyeur. I'm not exactly sure why I like watching Jaime make love to another woman. Each voyeur has their own highly developed reasoning. Since we gave up on prostitutes for good we've organized various threesomes, always in neutral territory, only with acquaintances or curious strangers.

Sometimes I watch Jaime and our special guest from a corner of the room, hidden in the darkness. With a timid hand I follow the rocking of their bodies, like stroking the back of a raging animal. They know I'm there, but I make myself invisible. I don't masturbate, I just watch, lusting in solitude and as I watch, I take over their bodies. As someone who doesn't particularly like being who she is, becoming someone else is thrilling.

Once we're alone, Jaime and I relive what happened. I try on their names, shapes, and the sound of their moans. I copy their movements in bed. I become someone else—I find a space to inhabit. I ask Jaime to call me by their names. Sometimes, in the middle of our game, Jaime takes my head, looks me in the eyes, and says my name: "Gabriela." And I start to cry without knowing why.

ISABEL ALLENDE WILL KEEP WRITING FROM THE AFTERLIFE

ON THE AFTERNOON of September 24, 2012, Isabel Allende died, and all the women who felt like they'd known her all their lives, as if each line that sprang from her pen had been written for them especially, lit scented candles on their bedroom altars and placed magic crystals around their copies of *Eva Luna*. My mother was one of them. Thousands of people connected to the internet at that time lamented the news, and the literary world readied itself to pay its hypothetical (and condescending) homage: "She possessed an unshakable vocation that led her to sell millions of books." Or, "more than a writer, she was a cultural phenomenon." But Allende had died on Twitter only, and a few minutes later she came back to life: "I am dying, but of laughter," she tweeted.

What would have been Allende's legacy if she'd died that September afternoon? A son, a husband, three grandchildren, a dog, a handful of bestsellers, and the belief held fairly unanimously by literary critics that the most widely read author in Spanish is a bad writer. It must be fun to have haters as prestigious as Bolaño or Poniatowska.

Isabel Allende is over seventy. Her death, therefore, is an immediate possibility, although, like the characters in some of her books, the author of *The House of the Spirits* does not see death as the end.

"I live knowing I'm experiencing only a fraction of reality," she told me the morning we met in Mexico. "There are thousands of dimensions to which we have no access."

Isabel Allende believes that anything is possible.

When she shows up at the airport in Mexico City, you can't stop thinking, however hard the more professional part of your brain might try, that Isabel Allende is far, far smaller than you'd imagined. She's dressed in black, wearing superlative heels, long earrings, gold necklaces, and a handbag that looks disproportionately big. She's very smart. She loves silk scarves, Indian tunics, and jewelry.

Very few writers manage to become celebrities, but she's famous enough to be on a par with the likes of Stephen King, Gabriel García Márquez, and J. K. Rowling. Meeting her split me in two: the more pedantic side of me aligned itself with the literary critics who denounce her hallowed writing, while the rest of me wanted to glory in the showbiz of being in her company.

We've been invited to a conference on *the intellectual experience of women in the twenty-first century*. She's speaking tomorrow night, and will have to arrive half an hour before her keynote speech to get her makeup done. "No one does my makeup," she says firmly, "they plaster it on like I'm a wall."

Seeing her in person is like settling in to watch a show, popcorn in hand: Isabel Allende acts as though the world were a stage upon which she, balanced on her impressive high heels, had placed a stool to bring her height up a bit more, as well as for comical effect. Within minutes she's declared: "I can still seduce my husband, as long as he's had three glasses of wine," "I had an erotic dream where Antonio Banderas was naked on a tortilla and covered in chili and guacamole," "I married a penis," and, on the way to the hotel, "Fortunately, I've got a husband, because otherwise I'd have to put ads up online. 'Short Latina granny over seventy seeks companion.' How awful! No one would answer." And she warns me she won't answer any of my questions until tomorrow.

In the car that picked us up at the airport, Allende gazes out at the suburbs of Mexico City and reminisces on her last visit to the country. I look at her profile against the window and think about posterity. For someone more afraid of disappearing than of dying, sitting next to her is like sitting beside an immortal being. I don't tell her this, of course, but as I sit there I'm also thinking that in some ways, Isabel Allende is like a mother to me. Like all mothers, she's a beloved female figure I'd hate to become. It might be the silk scarves, long earrings, and shamanic aura. Or perhaps I just don't want to become a seventy-something female author, which is inevitably what I will become.

I'm guessing I'm not the only one who started reading Allende because of their mother. I first saw the books on her bedside table. The only one I wasn't able to read at the time was *Paula* because Mom forbade me from doing so, though I did watch her read it with tears streaming down her face. My dad, on the other hand, gave me García Márquez so I'd appreciate great literature. Neither of these two schools of thought interfered with each other. I understood and enjoyed what each thing represented, and they've been located in different imaginative and emotional spaces ever since. Of course, though, while in college I obediently chorused "Isabel Allende is subliterature."

111

Sitting beside her while her car approaches the hotel, I feel increasingly tense. How to break the ice when she's asked me to be quiet? While we crawl through Mexico City's traffic, I hear myself ask:

"How tall are you?"

"Four foot nine," she replies. "Everyone's so tall nowadays. People were smaller when I was young."

And immediately afterward, Isabel Allende, the performer, monologist, and showgirl, adds: "The only place I feel good is in Thailand, because in the US, where I live, everyone's enormous. My grandkids are so tall." She says this with an intact Chilean accent that has retained its sharp musicality. "We have the same genes, so it must be the food. If I'm at a party, the only thing I can see is people's nose hair, and whenever someone's prawns slide off their plate, they always fall on me. It's hard being short these days." Now she's the one talking and asking me things. There's nothing foolish about her: the best way to stop someone asking questions is to interrogate them. She asks if I've got kids. I ask about her grandchildren. She asks me to show her a picture of my daughter on my phone. "How lovely!" she says. But she doesn't show me anything.

Isabel Allende is to literature what Shakira is to pop: they have a handful of fun, catchy hits with a somewhat dogmatic message and enough fans to fill stadiums. Pop, that expression of the ephemeral, makes Allende paradoxically everlasting. She gives the impression of taking her mission very seriously. She lives with the impunity only granted to those born with the gift of entertaining the masses. When anyone visits her mansion in California, where she writes, overlooking spectacular views of the San Francisco Bay, and asks her what she's planning on doing with the last years of her life, she always answers: "Carry on writing books." One can't be blamed for thinking that when she dies, Isabel Allende will keep writing from the hereafter.

Allende is an easy target for the canonizers of novels. It's possible that not many of her critics are willing to admit that the virulence of their attacks are based on prejudice: she's an upper-class woman who used to write a feminist column for a fashion magazine in the 1970s. At the age of forty, without any academic training, she started publishing novels, made autobiographical fiction her signature, and her books started flying off supermarket shelves. In a world where the stupidest things tend to be the most popular, sales of fifty million copies can only arouse suspicion.

But put yourself in her shoes: try having the surname Allende in Chile, going into exile, getting divorced, bringing up children, dedicating yourself to journalism, and writing novels. She was part of a generation of Latin American women who juggled all these things at once, and yet managed to triumph under the long shadow of the Boom—a movement that didn't really contain a single woman writer, only incredibly loving wives who kept everything nice and comfortable so that their husbands could finish their books and win that Nobel Prize.

Try writing from the bottom tip of the American continent about emotions and sex instead of tunnels and labyrinths. Now try to sustain a literary career over three decades with unwavering success. Try, moreover, to produce as many well-written novels as she has. Because Isabel Allende's books *are* well-written: there is a voice and an imagination. Isabel Allende builds her stories around simplicity. She occasionally succumbs to cheapness, lace, and frills, but her expression is founded on the richness of family stories, everyday comedy and drama, and the intimate knowledge of a feminine universe, as in *The House of the Spirits*. In *Eva Luna* or *The Infinite Plan*, being colloquial and inventive makes her prose even more personal and confessional. Her books reveal history through memory and reclaim sex so that it belongs to the home and not to poets of the body. In *Paula*, perhaps the best of her books, she describes a man's suffering in the presence of his comatose daughter's body. In it, the consciousness of being human reaches levels that Allende's language cannot match.

We know the outcome of Allende's adventure: few have built such a solid relationship with their readers, a relationship based on something mysterious and addictive that they find in her pages and which defies any logic outside itself. Isabel Allende isn't Virginia Woolf, she's not Clarice Lispector, and she's not Alice Munro; but neither is she a bestseller à la Dan Brown with his simple-minded esoteric vision of the crime novel. And yet he isn't criticized half as often as she is.

What's the sell-by date of a popular writer after the publication of their last hit? At this women-only conference I've heard names I hadn't heard for years: Laura Esquivel and Ángeles Mastretta, for example. And the first thing I thought was "they're still alive?" Yesterday I saw Mastretta, the author of commercial bombshells such as *Tear This Heart Out* and *Lovesick*, gliding down the corridors of the Palacio de Bellas Artes with her dramatic cheekbones, her carefully coiffed hair, and her fragile movements, and it was like stepping back into the eighties. On Wikipedia, I discover that she's carried on publishing books. In the last two decades of the twentieth century, the books of these three women were labeled "women's literature," a kind of derivation of "true literature" with sugary, sentimental additives of which Allende is the highest-profile proponent. Following its initial golden years, "women's literature" seems to have fallen out of favor, and Allende alone has remained a bestseller. After the success of *Like Water for Chocolate*, Esquivel took refuge in a mansion in the outskirts of Mexico City, tried out being a member of parliament, and now facilitates workshops and publishes books in the style of *12 Steps to Happiness*. Years after that enormous cocoa feast, Allende wrote her own book about sex and cocaine: *Aphrodite*, a book where cooking recipes lead to love (also known as the kind of book that immediately banishes you from the annals of Literature).

The next morning, I meet up with an immaculate Isabel Allende at a hotel lounge over American-style breakfast. We get to talking about why women identify so much with her stories and with their optimistic vision of the world, which places relationships and emotions at the forefront. When I bring up the topic of her critics, she replies as she always does: "women's writing" is a term used derogatively, and she's fought for years against this segregation. I'm intrigued to learn how she feels when judged not by a critic, which is bearable, but by another writer, especially when those authors enjoy great prestige.

"I take criticism like I take success," she says in a tone that changes from personable and offhand to forceful and proud. "Curiously, Elena Poniatowska doesn't say things about other writers. Why does she only say things about me? Because I sell books."

The executives staying in this hotel might well mistake Poniatowska's name for that of a Russian tennis player.

"Saying things about me makes her more visible. No one would ask Poniatowska what she thinks about my books if they weren't selling. Bolaño? He never said anything good about anyone. He was a good writer, but what a hateful man."

Bolaño called her an *escribidora*—a prolific and bad writer. Making fun of Isabel Allende isn't a sign of intelligence, it's part of Latin American literary folklore.

"There are people who say I'm a genius—do you think I lap that up? I've got work to do." Isabel Allende has turned serious. But not overly so.

It's true: Isabel Allende won't let anyone do her makeup. But this hint of rebellion speaks less to feminist ideals and more to her vanity. Allende does her own makeup because she looks better that way. I see her touching up her face in a compact mirror. In a few hours, she'll give her keynote speech at the Palacio de Bellas Artes in front of hundreds of people, including the president of Mexico and his wife. In half an hour, she'll give a live interview for a news show. She's wearing an orange blouse, a skirt, and a black cardigan. I tell her that she looks stunning—and mean it.

"I look great despite my age and it costs a fortune! But I'm not a slave to fashion," she clarifies. "The stupidity of women who think their lives will change with a different hair color annoys me."

Her hair is dyed a reddish brown and she pats her hands against the ends to create gentle curls, which she arranges over her ears. Today, as it happens, is International Women's Day, and being with Isabel Allende seems a fitting way of celebrating it. Her charitable foundation, whose projects support women, keeps her busy with conferences half the year.

"These female writers have so much power and so many resources," she goes on, "but instead of helping improve conditions for women, they smother them with aesthetic notions."

Allende says this with conviction. But her conviction didn't stop her from having surgery a few years ago. She had a face-lift and got rid of some wrinkles.

"So what? Of course I had plastic surgery. And I'd have more if I hadn't sworn to my son that I wouldn't do it again."

Isabel Allende talks about her only, spoiled son the same way one would talk about a jealous and controlling husband.

"My son doesn't even like me wearing makeup," she says. "But his influence has its limits."

The novelist, after all, was brought up in the '50s to be a good girl, and had to work hard to free herself through literature. Now she feels the need to justify her son and his aversion to makeup.

"He thinks it's vain. My daughter-in-law doesn't wear makeup, and look how pretty she is," she says, pointing across the room to the very thin, pale, and discreet woman that had accompanied Allende this whole time. She's Lori Barra, executive director of the Isabel Allende Foundation, wife of Nicolás Frías, and a kind of American alter ego who offers her a running commentary in English of everything that's happening. "She only goes to the hairdresser twice a year. That's my son: he likes simple and natural. I say to her 'Lori, you'd look even more gorgeous with a bit more lipstick on.' But he doesn't like it."

"And will you have more surgery?"

"Not right now, but maybe in five years I'll have my face done again. You have to be careful with plastic surgery, though, because what good is having your face stretched if everything else gives away your old age? There's nothing more ridiculous than those L.A. women who are stretched out like they've been ironed flat but who you can tell are ancient," she says.

Allende says she gave birth to her life philosophy back when she was working for *Paula*, a women's magazine that struck an unusual balance between frivolity and depth. "I learned how to be feminine, sexy, and a feminist. It can be done."

It's difficult to find writers who are dedicated readers of Isabel Allende. The day she received Chile's National Prize for Literature, some of her colleagues and fellow Chileans were outraged. The writer Alejandro Zambra, for example, said it was "like giving the Nobel to Paulo Coelho." Who will remember her work when she's not around? Who does Allende write for? Certainly not for the Argentinian Patricio Pron. The author of *The World Without People Who Ruin It and Make It Ugly* (how apt!) decidedly thinks Allende is not worth reading:

"Her books appropriate the most well-known methods and forms of the Boom—a literary and cultural project that was progressive at its outset—and put them at the service of a conservative vision of the world, according to which 'Latin Americanness' can only be experienced in one way, and if you're a woman only in the kitchen.

"It's as if Allende were one of those body snatchers from 1950s sci-fi films," he adds. "Or like a monstrous tapeworm or intestinal parasite that has eaten its host from the inside out."

If anyone compiled an anthology of *Great Moments in Criticism Against Isabel Allende*, it would surely include Pron's vision of a bloodsucking, parasitic writer. But to be fair, Allende's writing hasn't followed just one recipe: she did versions of magical realism in a couple of her books, and she has ventured into memoir, political and historical novels, and even children's books. It would be incorrect to lump her into romantic writing because, unlike Corín Tellado and her cohorts, the protagonists of Allende's fictions—among whom I'll include the author herself—are women who were revolutionary: they won their independence, read Simone de Beauvoir, and went on the pill.

I sent a dozen emails to authors to get their opinions on Allende. The truth is that I made a fairly simplistic calculation, cherry-picking profiles to get favorable opinions. Even the writers I believed were ideologically closest to Allende told me they either didn't read her work or hated it.

Santiago Roncagliolo, a "male writer" who has been vilified in Peru as if he were a "woman writer," and who has sold thousands of copies of his novel *Red April* replied with the following:

"In general, I respect bestsellers. It's not easy to move millions of readers around the world, and if someone manages to do so I respect them, even if they don't write the kind of books I enjoy reading."

Among Isabel Allende's extra-literary virtues, of which there are many, Roncagliolo focused on an admirable one:

"If there's something I really admire in her it's her ability to incite the hatred and envy of so many literary snobs. Of all Isabel Allende's work, the piece I most enjoy is the rage on the faces of the writers who think themselves eminent because no one wants to read them. Thank you, Isabel, for pissing them off."

Norman Mailer used to say that writing books with the conscious intent of them becoming bestsellers is not unlike marrying for money. Except it's hard to pull this off with books. A book can contain all the winning ingredients and still lose. Or it can be a potential loser and surprise everyone. This happened a couple of years ago with María Dueñas, a teacher from Spain who hadn't written a book in her life and became a bestselling author overnight. Her novel *The Seamstress* sold thanks to word of mouth— the publisher didn't spend one cent promoting it. Here's the juicy bit: this story of a Spanish seamstress who sets up a workshop in Morocco sold 1.5 million copies and was translated into twenty-seven languages. I asked Dueñas what she thought of Allende.

"I loved *The House of the Spirits* and I've followed her ever since it came out. I admire her talent and energy. She's a beacon in literature written by women, a huge inspiration, a teacher."

Dueñas really is a conscientious student, the new girl on the block of bestselling women writers in the Spanish-speaking world, those phenomena who sow novels and reap long queues of admirers. She's also the continuation of a particular way of understanding literary work. Dueñas, like Allende, uses literature to preserve an intimate, familiar, and collective memory. She's one of those documentary-makers of the heart who delve into and reshape the past in order to return it to the community in an accessible version—something that the market rewards with all its love. As if it were a simple task to write accessibly and earn millions.

*

Isabel Allende tells me she's a "cupid mother." Apparently, she was far from subtle when she intervened so that her son Nicolás and Lori Barra would meet.

"My poor, divorced son taking care of three children! He needed a woman," she exclaims. Allende's family stories are as extravagant as the sagas in her fiction. Nicolás's first wife, the mother of his three children, left him for another woman, the fiancée of one of Allende's husband's sons, no less. Now the children spend part of the time with their mothers and the rest of the time with Nicolás and his new wife. They all get on well and live near the matriarch's home, even her ex-husband, father of Paula, the daughter who died. Allende has borne not only her own suffering, but also that of her husband, whose family story is very tragic. His three children got into drugs: his daughter gave birth to a girl who is HIV positive, and then died of an overdose, and his two sons, now over forty, have spent their lives in and out of prison and rehab. *Maya's Notebook* is Allende's catharsis for this parental pain.

A day in the life of Isabel Allende:

She rises at six in the morning because her dog demands breakfast at that time. "My poor dog's old, too," she says. She's ten years old, the same age as Allende in dog years. At seven, her husband brings her a cup of tea. Then she meditates, exercises, and shuts herself in her "hovel" to work for six or seven hours. During that time, Willy Gordon writes, too. He's become a writer by association and even publishes his own books. From time to time, she goes out to see the view of the San Francisco Bay, and then goes back to writing. In the evening, they watch one of the films they still get from the rental shop. She answers emails, talks to Lori Barra.

For those of you who are into dates, 2012 was a year of milestones for Allende: she turned seventy and also celebrated thirty years since the publication of her first novel, *The House of the Spirits*, the book that earned her fame and fortune, as well as the stigma of having written an ersatz García Márquez novel. It was also twenty years since the death of her daughter. Her agent, Carmen Balcells, convinced her to write a memoir to help her grieve. *Paula* records the months she spent watching over her daughter while she was in a coma. Although she thought no one would want to buy a book about death, *Paula* has become the most enduring of all her books.

It's almost time for her keynote speech in the Palacio de Bellas Artes. Lori Barra looks very beautiful today, just as her mother-in-law said she would, wearing lipstick and a very flattering red dress. She's typing on her laptop, perhaps engrossed in work for the charitable foundation that Allende runs and which Lori helps administrate. While she's still busy with the press, I ask Allende how she gets on working with her daughter-in-law. Allende tells me that when she saw her she knew she was perfect for her son. She took her out on walks, just the two of them, to get to know her. It was only afterward that she knew she'd also be a reliable coworker. Your mother-in-law, your boss. It sounds like a nightmare. But Lori seems perfectly happy.

"Sometimes I forget she's my daughter-in-law," Allende says. "She's a great companion to me. She lives three blocks away. If I cook something Chilean, I send half of it over to her place. If she buys ripe tomatoes, she sends me half. We're closer than any real mother and daughter, because there's always more conflict there."

As we watch Lori working away, Allende tells me, "Sometimes I forget she's not my daughter, but she couldn't be: look how tall she is, and that face."

Isabel Allende visits her parents in Santiago de Chile twice a year. Ramón Huidobro, her stepfather, loves talking about her. When she was little, Isabel led an all-out campaign against him, but eventually he became a father to her. Huidobro hasn't inspired any of the characters in her books. "He is too decent and has too much common sense," Allende has written about him. "Novels are made of the demented and the villainous, of people tortured by obsessions, of victims of the implacable mills of destiny." Novels are made of characters such as her biological father, who was found dead in the street, and of whom the only memory she has is of his icy body in the morgue.

Uncle Ramón, as she calls Huidobro, is now almost a hundred years old. I ask him to define his stepdaughter in one word.

"She's an intellectual," he says on the other end of the line.

"But intellectuals aren't her biggest fans," I say.

"Because in this country people are full of jealousy. It's always been like that. Remember Neruda. That shows you how strange this country is."

I ask about his relationship with Allende.

"It's a father-daughter relationship, simple as that."

"Can you tell me a story about her?"

"I can't," he says in a strained, almost inaudible voice. "She's told so much that she's left nothing for me to tell."

*

Isabel Allende strokes her face and neck, as we women tend to do as if to check we haven't aged overnight. She prods her double chin. Soon she'll have to get ready for her talk. Perhaps because we haven't got much time together left, we talk about getting old.

"There's no glamour in getting old. There's a clear physical deterioration," she admits. "I no longer have the strength to do all the things I used to. I'm more selective, I don't waste time on stupid programs on the television or movies that don't teach me anything. If a book doesn't grab me by page thirty, I stop reading."

She says that her years of accumulated experience haven't helped her writing. In each book, she insists, it's important to reinvent everything so as to avoid making the same mistakes you already made. And the anxiety that comes with starting a new book is always the same.

"Why can't you waste time?"

"I can't waste it because time passes increasingly quickly," she says, and her eyes widen.

"But writers aren't like actresses who stop getting roles all of a sudden because they're getting older."

Isabel Allende admits that in a way getting older has been a blessing. Now she has more readers that she's won over with her work.

She's been on the verge of giving it all up several times, but she's convinced that literature is the one thing she couldn't do without. Even when writing is often torturous, Isabel Allende feels perfectly at ease.

"When I'm writing, I don't have to look good or be intelligent," she says, stifling her emotion, "or to captivate anyone."

Isabel Allende's sincerity is astounding. There's no topic she's too afraid to broach, including death, which is unusual in someone her age. But the woman who is not afraid of being "just a bestseller" is not afraid of death, either. A line from her novel *Eva Luna* would make for an appropriate epitaph for her: "There is no death. People only die when we forget them. If you can remember me, I will be with you always."

"My fear of death left me when my daughter Paula died. I watched her die, and a few days later my granddaughter was born. The moment of death is a lot like the moment of birth: it's a passage from one threshold to another."

She has said more than once that she doesn't care about posterity, she writes for the present. She's even prepared to be forgotten, for her novels to go out of fashion, and for a layer of dust to erase her footsteps more thoroughly than any of her critics. But some are skeptical. Carlos Franz, another Chilean writer and one of the few dissonant voices in the chorus of accusations, allowed her certain merits, but criticized her for trying to "hurry posterity along" by constantly complaining about the ostracism she faces:

"Even Isabel Allende will find her place—big or small—in the Pantheon of National Literature from which people exclude her today," said Franz.

"There's nothing terrible about death; what would be terrible is to live forever," Allende says. In *Paula*, she recalls a joke made by her father's first cousin, a then perpetual candidate for the presidency who was eventually elected in 1970. When asked what he'd like written on his epitaph, he replied: "Here lies the future president of Chile." One afternoon, uncle Salvador Allende was trying to teach his niece to shoot a bull's-eye with the same gun that would later be found beside him in the Palacio de la Moneda after he committed suicide. The young niece, after waving the gun in the air, ended up pointing it at the politician's head. The bodyguards ran and slammed her down to the ground.

Isabel Allende's parents are over ninety, and she lives knowing that any moment now, the phone will ring and she'll have to go back to Chile. In all these years, she hasn't stopped believing in ghosts and the power of memory and imagination to connect us with other worlds.

"Paula's always around," she tells me. "If I'm waiting for the elevator and it's taking too long, I say: come on, Paula, hurry this along."

The author of *The House of the Spirits* looks out of the large window at the dark Mexican sky that fiercely separates divinity from men.

"Wisdom isn't going to fall from the sky just because you get old," she warns me. "No. With age, unless you make an effort to grow, you're just more of what you always were."

Everyone knows that Isabel Allende has made thousands weep with her stories of love and darkness, but probably not many people know that she's also made people laugh. Years ago, during a time when the country was tinged with military green and blood red, she did so by writing a column published in the seventies bursting with feminist humor. Allende was writing *Civilize Your Troglodyte* years before we'd even dreamed of *Bridget Jones's Diary*, *Sex and the City*, or *Girls*. In it, she played a lead role in the now outdated war of the sexes, portraying men as inferior beings enslaved to their penises. It was a success, especially with men.

She's written books that are contrived and insufferable, but what author hasn't? And she's written the odd book that is both a moving testimony and the perfect blockbuster, like *Paula*, which at points has gotten me thinking that I would have liked to write it myself, albeit in a different way.

Do we really have to write like Clarice Lispector to warrant praise? As I do my research for this article, I begin to get so bored of reading a chorus of repeated charges that I decide I'm going to write dozens of articles that elevate Allende to Mount Parnassus. But then I say to myself, What the hell! She's a rich, famous, happy writer. She doesn't need anyone to defend her.

"You must be the worst journalist in this country, my girl," Pablo Neruda blurted at her when she went to his house at Isla Negra to interview him. "You're incapable of being objective, you put yourself at the center of everything, I suspect you lie a lot, and when you don't have news you make them up. Why don't you try writing novels instead? In literature those defects are virtues." Allende followed his advice and stopped being the outspoken journalist who handled sex, decorations, horoscopes, and recipes. "She was a die-hard feminist, but at six she ran home to attend to her husband like a geisha. And she gave us lessons on how to have it all!" her ex-boss, Delia Vergara, told me.

Sometimes, however, Isabel Allende's little journalism pieces turned very serious. Her most notable article was "An Interview with an Unfaithful Woman," the conversation she had with an upper-class woman married to an important politician who rented a room where she and two friends would meet their lovers. Priests condemned her; women loved her.

Allende soon found a niche that made her famous for a while: she played the lead role in her own "adventure-reportages," as she called them—a feminist gonzo journalist way ahead of her time. She once passed herself off as a dancer in a singles club. Her conservative compatriots nearly crucified her. Another time she was asked to write about LSD, and, of course, figured she might as well give it a try. But that was a long time ago. Nowadays, while some people busy themselves with the sad sport of mocking her, Allende has started writing her newest novel, as she does religiously every January 8. She's a hundred pages into a story that will be set in California.

On Isabel Allende's big night at the women's conference, the writer Sabina Berman introduced her by saying: "Isabel Allende's republic of readers is bigger than any Spanish-speaking country." When it's her turn, a man comes up to help her get the little stool on the stage in position. She climbs on the stool and begins her speech. She goes from jokes about herself to fables to parables— and from there to dramatic anecdotes. From lightheartedness to a devastating confession—and then to a sermon on cosmic feminine energy. "When women get together," she proclaims, "they are happy." She speaks to thousands of devoted women from around the world. The entire auditorium is putty in her capable hands. "My life has been marked by love. I still believe in a vision of life where love wins." The world is her stage. And her stories all stem from the same question: "What do women want?"

That is what all of us, men and women, want to know.

And she seems to have the answer.

EPILOGUE

THE IMPERFECT CRIME

Almost two years have gone by since Twitter falsely announced Isabel Allende's death, and at seventy-one, her career is still as nimble as ever. If the first novel she wrote in the eighties was about spirits, her most recent one is about cadavers. She is now making her debut in crime fiction with the aid of Google, to which she turns when she needs to know, for example, what factors affect the progression of rigor mortis.

Now it's 6 p.m. on a Thursday in January in Madrid, and the long day she's spent being interviewed about her new novel is almost over. By now it is quite likely that Allende is tired of listening to journalists or of talking altogether. But she turns out to be as enthusiastic as ever. The meeting takes place, fittingly, in the decadent suite of a hundred-year-old hotel that has one hundred and fifty rooms. In it, scenes taken from different eras play out simultaneously: Lori works silently in the bedroom on her laptop, while her mother-in-law sits in the living room surrounded by Belle Époque luxury. Where Ernest Hemingway once wrote in his boxer shorts and Grace Kelly and Rainiero celebrated their honeymoon, Isabel Allende now serves tea and assorted biscuits.

"I know you. We met at . . . " she leaves the phrase hanging, waiting for my help to complete it. "Oh, at the women's conference, right?"

A year and a half ago, Isabel Allende was dominating the world atop that little stool at the feminist gathering. Now she's staying at a hotel where up until 1975, the year dictator Francisco Franco died, women wearing pants were denied entry.

"Would you be a minister in Michelle Bachelet's government?" I ask her, referring to the Chilean president she so admires.

"I'd be no good at that. I'd be as clueless as if you asked me to iron your shirt. I've got no idea how to do it."

I remind her that Vargas Llosa, in his Nobel acceptance speech, said that his wife used to tell him: "Mario, the only thing you're good at is writing."

"A man can allow himself the luxury of only being good at writing. I love writing, but I have to do many other things."

Although she spends time doing other things, she never misses her January eighth appointment with a new novel. And she always manages to make her new books "on trend." Some might say that she always jumps on the bandwagon of other bestsellers, but Allende believes she has the talent of sensing a sort of collective consciousness, which she then speaks to in book form. She did this with magical realism, with dictatorship novels, with stories of love and cooking, with the Harry Potter saga when she stepped into children's fiction, and she's done it again with crime fiction. Allende swears to me she didn't know crime fiction had become trendy; however, before writing her own, she prepared by devouring Stieg Larsson's *Millennium* trilogy—as she likely devoured *One Hundred Years of Solitude* in the eighties. When she finished the trilogy she knew that however hard she tried, she would never be able to write anything in Larsson's style. It would be pointless to even try.

"It's too brutal, too dark, that's not how I see life. So I set out to write a crime novel my way."

And thus *Ripper* was born—a "crime" novel, or more precisely a novel meant "to poke fun at other crime novels." *Ripper* tells the story of a talented, dreamy girl, inspired by Allende's granddaughter, who loves virtual role-playing games and sets out to uncover the real identity of an avatar, Jack the Ripper, who is responsible for a series of real-life crimes. To do so, the girl enlists her helpful grandfather.

Allende says that if she'd grown up with the internet, as her granddaughter has, she would never have overcome her shyness or found feminism, and nor would she have become a writer.

"I know that serial killers are terrible, hateful beings," she suddenly exclaims, "and you shouldn't joke about them, but fiction is fiction."

Maybe Isabel Allende didn't realize that crime fiction was on trend because, in her house, it always has been. The person responsible for this is her American husband Willy C. Gordon, reader and writer of crime fiction.

"I was telling him that I was going to start *Ripper* with a description of the neighborhood in San Francisco where it would all take place, and Willy shouted in horror: 'No! A crime novel starts with a dead body! You have to start by killing someone.' That had never occurred to me."

I wonder if the Twitter hoax about her own death wasn't also the start of a novel. A novel we all wrote and that revolves around the corpse of Isabel Allende. For decades, she has been the subject matter of so many a murderously vindictive colleague that it wouldn't be strange if she really were a ghost wandering around talking about crimes and bodies.

"How long does it take for a body to go into rigor mortis?" I ask her, to check whether she'd done her homework.

"It all depends on the temperature. There are lots of things I researched on Google about poison and weapons only to forget them five minutes later. Why go through life with corpses and crimes rattling around in my mind? When I need another body, I'll find it online again."

The woman sitting next to me in a suite in the Madrid Ritz may be a woman of a certain age, but she'll never be a ghost. Unfortunately for her critics, both life and death smile on Allende.

How long will Isabel Allende be around in this world or the next?

It all depends on the temperature.

A TRIP THROUGH AYAHUASCA

WE LOOK LIKE FUNERAL BUNDLES dug out from our graves.
A dozen or so people sitting stiffly in a circle on the floor in
the room, in the dark. In the center of our circle sits the healer.
He smokes a *mapacho*, a roll of tobacco leaves, and blows the
smoke over the neck of a bottle full of viscous liquid. He takes
a sip, then calls us to him one by one. I'm scared. People who've
taken ayahuasca say it tastes disgusting and the initial effects—
stomachache, nausea, dizziness, and shivering—are hard to bear.
Everyone says a quick prayer and drinks unflinchingly. I go last.

Days earlier, the healer had instructed me to follow a prepara-
tory diet: I had to abstain from pork, fats, spicy food, alcohol,
pills, and sex—all of which, he said, would neutralize the effect
of the plant. But there was more: a night before the session, I
found myself vomiting alongside a group of strangers who, just
like me, had ingested an Amazonian brew and eight liters of
water in order to expel the toxins that the "western world had
left in our bodies." The "purge," as the healers call it, is the final
step before taking ayahuasca, and it is almost as important as the
ayahuasca itself. The concoction we drank consisted of tobacco
leaves, several flowers, and various vomit-inducing plants.

From time to time, and leaving me scandalized, the healer
came over to examine the contents of our vomit and diagnose
all manner of ailments: from stress to renal colic.

I'd arrived early at the address I'd been given. How could the invisible forces of nature be summoned in this upper-class, gated neighborhood? It had to be a scam. In a move that put an end to my idealized notion of an authentic, magic, selfless shaman, I'd paid the healer an equivalent of forty dollars for an experience that is purportedly priceless.

But I'm here, I've taken the drink, and there's no turning back. All I feel is stomach pain and an immense eagerness to leave. I'm not seeing anything yet. Some people have started vomiting. The visions are supposed to come after you vomit.

Back in my university days, whenever I heard about ayahuasca it always seemed to be shrouded in mystery. (And in bullshit, I thought.) One of my best friends' mothers was an anthropologist, and every so often, a healer would lead a session in my friend's living room. My friend used to turn up to our class on Kantian philosophy and tell me that the previous night she'd turned into a leopard, flown over Medieval Europe, and discovered that she spoke Mandarin. I asked her to invite me as nonchalantly as if I were asking for a joint, to which she replied: "I don't think you're ready yet." According to her, ayahuasca was life-changing and not a drug for those merely hoping to trip on psychedelic visions of magical serpents and flashing colors.

I later learned that a lot of people use the visions it induces to explore their inner worlds, traumas, and issues—a plant-based psychotherapy of sorts. A woman once told me that though religion had been the first to introduce her to the concept of God, ayahuasca was to thank for introducing her to God in person. A man said he'd been able to sort out some unfinished business with the souls of his dead relatives. Others claimed to have seen distant ancestors. According to various accounts, drinking ayahuasca allowed them to traverse large distances and different epochs. For some, ayahuasca revealed their mission in this world and the faces of their unborn children. Others discovered unknown talents—anything from singing and knitting to solving complex formulas.

What everyone had in common was a revelation—they had all heard a voice that answered their questions. I was keen to ask some questions of my own, but on this occasion, the only thing in store for me was a touch of nausea and the feeling of being stoned. Disillusioned, I left at dawn.

Ayahuasca is a substance believed capable of channeling telepathic powers, used by indigenous healers to seek lost objects, particularly "bodies and souls." In the rainforest they call it "madrecita ayahuasca" because they believe the plant has a sort of feminine wisdom. In Quechua, ayahuasca means "rope of the dead," an allusion to its ability to connect us with another dimension. The concoction known as ayahuasca is a mixture of two plants: the liana (ayahuasca) and either *chacruna* or *toé*—both of which contain the substance known as dimethyltryptamine (DMT), which is present in the human brain and may be involved in the production of dreams. Healers boil both these plants to make the thick brew. This substance is more visionary and entheogenic than simply hallucinogenic or psychedelic. Ingesting it doesn't alter the senses; it produces a state of ecstasy, coupled with an intuition of what is deep and transcendent.

In Brazil, there are three syncretic religions that regularly use ayahuasca in their liturgies as a way to access the divine. In the indigenous communities in the rain forest, shamans drink ayahuasca to detect ailments and cure them. Hundreds of years ago, and without having read a single book on botany, indigenous people were well-versed in the properties of plants and their infinite combinations.

The effects of ayahuasca have also been tested in the treatment of addictions. There is a therapeutic community in Peru that treats cocaine and ecstasy dependence with ayahuasca. It is also used to astounding success to combat anxiety and severe depression, as a complement to chemotherapy, and to treat people with AIDS.

But how can we explain the less easily documentable telepathic phenomena, the ability to communicate with ancestors, or the feeling of oneness with the Universe? Jeremy Narby, a Swedish anthropologist, enthusiastically puts forth the idea that the coiled double snake, an image central to shamanic lore, is an Amazonian synonym for the DNA helix. Based on this assertion, he hypothesized that ayahuasca could help glimpse genetic information that reveals our origins and our future.

Before taking ayahuasca for the first time, I read *The Yage Letters*, the letters that William Burroughs sent in 1953 to his disciple, the poet Allen Ginsberg, from Panama, Ecuador, Colombia, and Peru. In them, he narrates his journey through the jungle in search of ayahuasca, known in Colombia as yagé. Burroughs was seeking "the ultimate high" after having tried heroin, marijuana, and cocaine. The book also contains Ginsberg's reply, written seven years later from Peru, which describes his own visions and terrors with the same plant, and asks Burroughs for advice.

Ginsberg writes: "I felt like a snake vomiting out the universe—or a Jivaro in head-dress and fangs vomiting up in realization of the Murder of the Universe—my death to come—everyone's death to come. . . . The whole hut seemed rayed with spectral presences all suffering transfiguration with contact with a mysterious Thing that was our fate and was sooner or later going to kill us." Ginsburg breaks down, remembering his mother, who died in a distant place, perhaps in pain, and decides to have children, a revolutionary act in his life.

"Too horrible for me, still—to accept the fact of total communication with say everyone an eternal seraph male and female at once—and me a lost soul seeking for help," wrote the beatnik. His experience, it appears, was full of fear. I know of people to whom the voice of ayahuasca has told great jokes, and in an instant shown them their dead children. As the shaman says to Ginsberg, "the more you saturate yourself with Ayahuasca the deeper you go—see the moon, see the dead, see God—see Tree Spirits."

The idea of a white man going into the remote depths of the South American jungle in search of a powerful psychotropic plant has by now become a trope. Increasingly, shamans are taking ayahuasca to big cities, traveling by plane throughout the world at the summons of rich people. If Burroughs had been a beatnik of the new millennium, he wouldn't have needed to leave the filthy couch in his junkie room.

According to popular belief, to take the plant in the city is to take it out of its ritual context, and to do so without the protection of a shaman's knowledge is dangerous. A friend of mine, a young poet, had been taking it alone for some time when he locked his room, doused his body with gasoline, tied his legs to his bed, and set himself on fire. I saw him a few days before he died. He had a strange expression, something that verged on happiness.

My ticket is bought, my bags are packed—and I've got my period. I've been told you can't take ayahuasca while menstruating since the "contaminating waste" of menstruation "disrupts the plant's vigor." And there I was thinking ayahuasca was female. I go anyway.

An hour and a half flight takes me to Pucallpa, ayahuasca paradise, where I meet up with Miguel Ángel, a journalist friend. We dream we're Burroughs and Ginsberg reincarnated, and wonder how we'll find the right shaman. We've been told a shaman is a necessary ceremonial intermediary between the plant and its enthusiasts. Unlike doctors in white coats, traditional healers take into account each person's internal life. They travel to the realm of the invisible, ascend to a divine plane, and speak to the energies that are ailing us.

But sometimes we forget that shamans are people, just like us. Some of the most famous shamans, sucked in by the system, have uprooted their forest huts to plush European hotels, where they hold expensive ayahuasca sessions. But what's really worrying are the *maleros*, healers who've fallen into darkness. Malero hexes might take you for a ride, and you don't want a demon driving. Of course, not all shamans are like this. To become a shaman, initiates spend months in the jungle dieting strictly to learn the powers of each plant. In their ayahuasca-induced trance, they must allow themselves to be devoured by the spirits of ferocious animals.

A friend had recommended that we find Rosendo Marín, a healer whose pure spirit "radiates goodness." I'm tempted to agree with everyone who'd told me Pucallpa is the ugliest city in Peru—a huge market miles away from the forest. The air is savage: hot, invasive, and sticky. We check into a hostel and head toward Yarina. Our plan is to find Rosendo in the indigenous community of San Francisco de Yarinacocha, interview him, and ask if he'll conduct a session for us the following night. It's nearly nighttime, however, and there are no more boats leaving for San Francisco until tomorrow. Someone suggests we travel by land, but at the bus stop all the drivers are asleep, slumped over their steering wheels.

A short distance away, we see why: an enormous metal animal lies gravely wounded in the middle of the road. A few days ago, heavy rainfall washed away the bridge connecting Yarina and San Francisco, and the desolate road is now impassable. I can't help but wonder if this is symbolic. After all, ayahuasca is the bridge to other dimensions.

Resigned, we head back to the hotel, but take one last look at the boats coming in from San Francisco. A man shouts: "boat trips, boat trips, boat trips to nature reserves" and then, to our surprise, "consultations with shamans." He turns out to be an expert tour guide who knows all the local shamans. Except, of course, for Rosendo. He tells us the famous shaman Guillermo Arévalo lives in Yarina. We take a mototaxi whose driver knows where Arévalo lives. We knock several times to no avail and are about to leave when a black SUV stops outside the door. A beautiful mestiza woman steps out; the taxi driver tells us she's Guillermo's wife. She happened to come by to pick up a few things. No, he's not in, they're staying over at their lodge in Soi Pasto. At this point it doesn't seem like sheer luck that we ran into her. Are we being beckoned by some kind of power? The woman tells us we can come, but we'll only have an hour to interview Guillermo because he's starting a session at nine. It will be a difficult night, she tells us. He has to cure an aunt who's suffering from cancer.

During the five-mile ride to the lodge in the same mototaxi, the driver tells us about the SUV, a gift given to the shaman by a gringo, and about the road built exclusively to get to the lodge, which must have cost "shitloads." When we arrive, the light of a paraffin lamp greets us. It's him. With a calm smile he beckons us in. Either he was told by a spirit we were coming, or his wife called him on his mobile. A matter of faith.

Guillermo is a fascinating person: he studied in Brazil, is an itinerant shaman who travels all over the world, and has acted in several Swedish and Dutch films. At the end of our conversation, he invites us to take part in the ceremony. Breaking with our plan fills me with dread. I try to tune into my intuition for guidance—but my normally overzealous inner voice is silent. Miguel Ángel is convinced we should do it. In the end, I accept. He leads us into a cabin that was built, Guillermo tells us, on a spot that had been struck by lightning. At one end, the ailing woman is lying on a large cot suspended from ropes. She's covered from head to toe with sheets.

I don't know whether to tell the shaman I have my period. By this point, I am neck deep in the whole thing and seriously concerned my menstrual energies might turn destructive and damage the shaman's power. I've heard shamans can even read women's energies and discern if they're being dishonest. Feeling guilty, I go over to Don Guillermo and whisper: "Maestro, I'm menstruating, can we carry on?" The shaman puts on a grim face, then nods and lets me decide. I take my seat and ready myself for the trip.

I see a frightening spectacle of dead animals, decomposing fetuses, and theatrical rapes. The sick woman pokes her head out from among the white sheets and I think hers is the face of someone I love, but disfigured by cruelty and reproach. Is this because of my period? Miguel Ángel won't stop singing nursery rhymes and crying like a madman, and in my trance I'm convinced he's weeping over the rotting body of my aborted baby. Then I'm being chased through a ruined city, jumping over streams of mangled, bloodied bodies. The Cashinahua people believe that fear is good for expelling negative energies and healing, but I can't understand what could possibly be helpful about this. It occurs to me that this man is a malero. I've been lured in by the darkness.

I wake up slowly. I stand up and look for the shaman, but he's nowhere to be seen. I have the feeling I'll never get out of here. Hours pass, but the darkness outside only seems to thicken. Miguel Ángel is quiet, radiant, and thankful. He's like a newborn bathed in placenta, while all I can think of is blood and black magic. I start to feel as though the cabin is a coffin. They've bricked us in, I'm sure of it. We're dead and death is this desperate insomnia.

It's a bad trip, like a flirtation with madness. I start seeing brilliant white figures moving among the trees. I wonder if I'm still hallucinating, but no, my eyes are open, and the figures must be the blessed spirits of the forest, heralding dawn. As soon as it starts to get light out, I launch myself at the door. Obsessed with the idea of the cabin-coffin, I'm nearly shocked to death when a huge black dog jumps in my way and, barking aggressively, blocks the exit.

Miguel Ángel and I manage to get out of the cabin. There's no one around. The shaman and his wife are sleeping in another cabin. In silence, we slip a few notes under their door as payment for the night's work and cross the small farm. Miguel Ángel wants to go back to the hotel, but I insist we have to look for Rosendo. We get into a boat that quickly takes us to San Francisco Island. The tension between us is unbearable. We don't speak. I lose myself in the pattern of the sun refracting on the water. During the trance, we'd cried and confessed things to each other, secret and shameful truths, and now something seems to have broken between my friend and I. The delirious nightmare seems unending. We argue about Arévalo. Miguel Ángel admires him, whereas I feel as if I were fleeing the malero to seek my true healer, Rosendo, who I'm certain will cure my imaginary woes. This second trip has left me untethered and paranoid. People say ayahuasca is the jungle's TV set, and I need to switch channels before turning it off.

As soon as we disembark in San Francisco, the locals try to put me off searching for Rosendo. A man tells me that he is out drinking somewhere on the island. Although it seems incredible, shamans tend to rob one another of their clientele in squabbles over supernatural turf. I think about the destroyed bridge, the black dog, the horrible visions. A strange energy is preventing me from meeting Rosendo.

Eventually, though, I manage to find him. He's not drunk—he's rocking his youngest daughter gently in a hammock. This image seems both an ending and a beginning. It occurs to me that this peace has been awaiting me since the beginning. I tell Miguel Ángel I intend to stay the night in Rosendo's hut. My friend thinks it would be enormously stupid to stay by myself in the jungle. He asks me one last time if I'm sure, and then leaves.

I look around me. I've traded an opulent lodge for a modest hut with no electricity. Rosendo's plot of land is seeded with the visionary plants I'm about to ingest. Night falls and the healer receives his guests. He gives me my dose of ayahuasca and guides me toward the hut. I close my eyes without fear.

Finally: my arteries and veins are growing and curling like creepers, so taut they feel as though they're about to snap. I can see my innermost body and hear the constant beating of my organs, a primitive lullaby. I watch the pathways that traverse my body, bathed in a greenish-gold liquid energy that runs from the crown of my head to my toes. I feel deeply happy and at the same time powerfully guilty that I'd ever doubted the plant's curative powers. I chastise myself for my relentless skepticism, my pedantic sarcasm, my unfettered cynicism. I cry at my unbearable arrogance, at my prized illusion of control. But even while I'm mercilessly berating myself, a voice whispers, "how paralyzing, this self-pity"—and I decide to forgive myself. I even begin to laugh out loud, joyfully.

I become a seed so small and modest I nearly disappear. I've never felt so whole, so uncensored, so compassionate. This freedom is accompanied by a sensation of physical well-being. All of a sudden, it's clear to me why some people say taking ayahuasca is like instant, accelerated psychoanalysis. A sensation of peace overcomes me, and I think I become aware of a higher power.

I'm awake, and can hear the birds, the shaman's songs, and the sounds of Rosendo's children nearby. Everything turns blue, a color that supposedly indicates bad spirits have exited my body. I talk to family and friends, both living and dead. I apologize to anyone I've ever betrayed or been unkind to. While I meditate on this, I hear an ancient voice—is it the ayahuasca's or is it my own? It answers questions firmly, but is as sweet and consoling as a mother. I ask questions about my present, past, and future, and it answers me. I start to feel weightless. My soul hovers over me, and I feel as though I could forever leave this burdensome body, which I watch writhe in bewilderment and fear.

I see Rosendo singing beautiful, comforting songs, blowing on my head with protective tobacco smoke.

I'm the last to get up. I'm blinded by the light. Rosendo Marín's wife is making clay pots, his daughters are nursing his grandchildren, and the older kids are chasing lizards. I emerge from the mosquito net as if from a white uterus, exhausted but happy.

GOODBYE, LITTLE EGG, GOODBYE

AT THIS PRECISE INSTANT, a child of mine is growing inside an unknown woman. I need to find another way to refer to it. It's not technically my child, even though it carries all my genetic information. While I was going through the donation process, the doctors called it Little Egg. Last I heard, Little Egg got transformed into an embryo after being swirled in a test tube with the semen of a man I will never sleep with, and who is the husband (or not) of this unknown woman. Little Egg then set up camp inside this unknown woman, where it must be cozy and warm.

Approximately half a year ago, I went to one of Barcelona's private assisted reproduction clinics to offer myself up as a donor, following the instructions given to me by some women I'd interviewed for an article about donating eggs. They were all young Latin American women like myself. They had come to Spain to study, and they all held casual jobs waitressing or handing out flyers. Most of them had found out about egg donation through posters—which the clinics put up at universities to attract young educated women—and had been drawn in by the enticing sum of nine hundred euros printed in red at the bottom of the flyer. I decided to undergo the donation process myself, and one summer morning walked into a clinic in an affluent upmarket neighborhood.

As soon as she took one look at me, the doctor politely shook my hand and said: "I don't want to waste your time." Her words were, and I quote: "We have no demand for . . . exotic eggs. Couples want eggs from girls who look like them. They want to avoid rumors. Imagine what would happen if the child inherited your eyes or black hair. People might think it's the child of the local—bank clerk." I realized she'd caught herself before saying something else. "Privacy is paramount here. Otherwise, couples would just adopt a Vietnamese kid."

The majority of clients in these clinics are Caucasian Europeans. Many are Spanish, but they also come in droves from countries such as Denmark, Switzerland, Germany, and Norway, where assisted reproduction is not allowed. The doctor looked at me like I was selling encyclopedias, said "we'll call you," and took down my information and ethnic characteristics ("American Indian features"). Her explanation seemed logical, although I couldn't help but think that my future offspring were facing racial discrimination before they'd even been born.

Soon after, while I was doing my shopping at the supermarket, I heard a radio ad cheerfully inviting women to become donors at the Dexeus clinic. I wound up at the clinic's doors for a second, more successful attempt at donating eggs. In the waiting room, I read the information leaflet: "The law on assisted reproduction determines that the donation must be free of charge." The concept of "financial compensation"—the politically correct term for the sale of eggs—was introduced ten years ago, and it broke new ground for the hundreds of women with fertility problems who languished on waiting lists and paid around nine thousand euros per fertility treatment. From that moment on, clinics started promoting egg donation left, right, and center.

Who are these women? I wonder, looking around the clinic. Aside from having dysfunctional or nonexistent ovaries, they seem to enjoy reading *Hello* magazine in waiting rooms. They are accompanied by either a man or another woman. Some are young, others are much older. Married, single, straight, or gay, they come from all over Europe, harbingers of Spain's "reproductive tourism boom." I am one of the donors: women under thirty-five, usually Latin American, blessed by nature with healthy ovaries. I'm an entry in the catalog, a hair color, a weight, a dress size, a blood type, an ID photo. I intend to use the money to pay off the last installment of my master's degree in Cultural Communication. I'm the archetypal, dutiful Latin American donor.

Tatiana, a Brazilian girl sitting opposite me, came to Barcelona a year ago to study and work, but because of the six-month-old baby in arms, only her husband can work now. She's hoping to make some much-needed extra cash. "I don't know if they'll accept me, they still have to run a bunch of tests. It's a long process." Her anxious face makes me worry.

There are no statistics, but doctors specializing in assisted reproduction estimate that at least 15 percent of the donors are Latin American, although I suspect the figure could be twice as high. According to the clinic's Dr. Montse Boada, neither nationality nor race are reasons for exclusion, "but it's true that not all recipients accept certain donors. We have to inform them. That's just the way it is. We don't live in a multiracial society." According to Dr. Ricardo Coroleu, however, some women are delighted to use a Latin American egg like mine.

Recipients and donors share the same room—we look at each other and need each other, but we don't know each other. The process is, by law, anonymous. The woman who'll get Little Egg might, unbeknownst to both of us, be sitting in this very room.

Today I'll receive the test results. Two months have passed since my first appointment. I've seen the gynecologist, the biologist, the psychologist. I've been pricked with a thousand needles to rule out AIDS and hepatitis and to profile my genetic karyotype. I've completed an interminable psychology test designed to detect any psychiatric pathologies, and they've made me sign a form in which I agree, among other things, to never stake a demented maternal claim over Little Egg.

I get the green light; I can't believe it. From here on, the biologist, a young woman with glasses and short hair, will supervise me during the hormonal treatment. What will my recipient make of me? It amuses me to imagine myself as a hen laying golden eggs. The egg retrieval has been scheduled for mid-December, less than a month from now. The biologist has written a fastidious "ovary hyperstimulation program," which is synchronized with the recipient's menstrual cycle. In the days prior to the donation, I have to come off the pill and be extremely cautious when it comes to sex, or I might get pregnant with triplets. To top things off, I'm constantly in a foul mood, and feel as though I'm having five intense periods all at once.

Every morning I leave home very early and take the train to the clinic. There, a stocky nurse with a matter-of-fact expression stabs me with an intramuscular injection to stimulate my levels of estradiol, the hormone that produces eggs. My butt punctured and my dignity crushed, I return the next day to take a blood test and get an ultrasound. "They're still quite small," the ultrasound technician says, unimpressed. When she leaves me by myself, I glance at the black screen.

I gawk, losing myself in cosmic reverie. They're planets surrounded by brightness. Each egg looks like a perfectly still drop of black water, almost a Zen puddle. These are the precious little eggs worth nine hundred euros that the medical staff fatten like they're pigs in a farmyard.

I get tired of the plumping my eggs undergo every day. On the tenth day, the gynecologist issues his verdict: "They're top-notch." I've got ten mature and chubby eggs, almost the size of a cherry, ready to be transported. That's why I'm bloated and finding it difficult to walk. The night prior to the operation, Jaime tucks me in. I dream I have a child with him, but when the nurse brings it to me it's not a baby but a smiling egg. Today, when I leave the operating room, I'll be handed a check that now seems like a pittance considering what I've had to endure. I feel like the most altruistic person on the planet.

I'm taken to room eleven on the ground floor. I make the most of the time I'm kept waiting by snooping around the corridor, just in case I catch sight of the recipient. When I come out of the operating room, the doctor will tell her how many little eggs are available. A man will then go into the bathroom with a dirty magazine and play his part. Before dawn tomorrow, Little Egg will have been fertilized in a cold, dark laboratory. On the second or third day, the embryo will already be mature enough to be transferred to the recipient. I don't see anyone who might be her, but I do see another donor being wheeled out of surgery. She is demonstrably Latin American and she is asleep. She looks pale. I'm scared.

The procedure will start with a follicular puncture. That means they'll use a needle to extract the little eggs through my vagina while the doctor follows the procedure from her ultrasound screen. They'll have to knock me out like a log. They'll retrieve around ten little eggs, use half, and freeze the rest in an embryonic state. The whole thing takes around thirty minutes.

A nurse comes in to wheel me through to the operating room. A woman dressed in green scrubs puts a shower cap on me, another woman spreads open my legs, a third inserts the needle for the IV drip in my hand, and the anesthetic runs its course. When I wake up, the first things I see are Jaime's worried face and a glass of orange juice.

I feel very uncomfortable over the next few days, as though I've gone against my body's nature. But the feeling passes, it becomes a distant memory, as the doctors had promised. Today, my ovaries and I are back to normal. I read in a paper that in the UK there's been a law in force since 2005 by which donors lose their right to be anonymous. Once the children of these donors turn eighteen, they have the right to find out who their biological parents are. I imagine myself opening the door eighteen years from now to find Little Egg dressed in jeans and a polo shirt and sporting a bushy beard. Or with long, shiny black hair and skinny jeans—looking at me with curiosity, the way I would.

Then, I feel sad and think it's possible Little Egg didn't survive the trip. But maybe it did, and somewhere there's a couple expecting a child with American Indian features. Or maybe it's an embryo that has been frozen for cloning research and will one day save humanity. In my favorite version of Little Egg's story, though, it's a tiny body traveling toward the light.

Sleep well, Little Egg.

WAITING FOR 11/11/11

1

SEVEN YEARS HAVE PASSED since this happened. It was in 2007, my year of full-time motherhood, when the job offer that should've come didn't and it was easier to retreat than to keep trying. Back then, I didn't know that one day I would be able to proudly say I'd breast-fed and cared for my daughter full-time during her first year of life. The only thing I knew at the time was that my existence had come to a screeching halt. Being a writer seemed ridiculous, I had no mission other than attending to what my baby signaled every day with her noises and with the smell of her diaper. It's no coincidence—indeed in this tale nothing is a coincidence—that this was also the year when the number 11 cropped up so often in my life that its insistent presence became nearly unremarkable.

I glance at the clock and there it is—11:11. It happens to me all the time, day and night. Every time it happens I tell Jaime, who, because I've been showing him concrete proof all these years, has ended up believing it's not just a fantasy of mine. I call it "my stupid secret." He calls it "your thing."

This is not at all like refusing to walk under a ladder or avoiding crossing paths with a black cat. Superstitions are collective, harmless nonsense that some people pay heed to in case the fools are right. But the thing with the number 11 is that a part of me, likely the obsessive-compulsive part, enjoys the thought that this is an external force that decided to pursue me. Seeing the number 11 transports me from cheerfulness to experiencing a feeling of enigmatic complicity with myself.

It's possible that my mind was feverish for most of 2007. I swept floors, washed clothes, and stirred the soup while I had a baby strapped to my back, barely slept, hardly had any sex, and couldn't remember the last film I'd watched or book I'd read. I was hardly a human being. During the years I devoted to child-rearing, to being a textbook woman—and a 1950s textbook at that—I swear that my appointments with the pediatrician always fell on the 11th. If I got on a plane I was given seat 11C. I was eleventh in the queue at the bank. Or my new ID card expired on the 11th.

My life, as I say, was suddenly devoid of research, journalism, and even literature. Like in the book by my beloved Joan Didion, it was "a year of magical thinking." The boundaries between superstition, faith, and madness were blurred. I lived with the certainty that an act or word of mine could have colossal repercussions. In my pre-scientific state, people rose from their graves, birds knew it was the end of the world, and numbers contained messages.

2

It was well past 11 a.m.—I know it was because at noon I tended to head back from the play park hoping to take advantage of Lena's nap time to take a shower—when I spoke to the witch for the first time.

As we all know, play parks are astral portals. On the few mornings when I didn't feel like an insect trapped in a spiderweb of dirty dishes, scattered toys, and unfolded laundry, when I wasn't irreparably sleep-deprived and despondently contemplating the prospect of having to get lunch ready in an hour while entertaining Lena with my tits—or rather, on the few mornings when all of the above still existed but I was able to stuff it in the depths of Lena's stroller and slam the door behind me—I would head for the park. Mooring the stroller outside the artificial beach with swings and sandboxes was like clocking into an unknown dimension. Taking my small child out to get fresh air and interact at ground level with her contemporaries was a cosmic achievement. Teaching her that the bird on the sidewalk was a pigeon? A PhD dissertation in biology. Stopping her from eating dirt? A heroic feat.

I began to move like a weightless astronaut in a universe of babies who still couldn't hold up their own heads, who were accompanied by either their Latina babysitters or their Catalan grannies. It was one of those babysitters, a red-haired girl looking after a Chinese boy, who introduced me to the witch. The woman, who must've been at least seventy-five years old, with long, gray hair and a flowy dress, was versed in astrology, metaphysical matters, extraterrestrials, and all things New Age. A charlatan to anyone else and a powerful witch to a bored mother in the park.

"Do you know why I keep seeing the number 11 everywhere?"

She looked at me from behind her enormous glasses and commended my soul to God.

"11," she said, "guides the lives of certain very special people who are called on to make great sacrifices during their time in this world."

I, who had already spent several months as a martyr, looked at her scornfully.

"The people around you," she went on, "depend on you. When the time comes, you'll have to protect them. The number 11 will guide you away from evil and toward good. You belong to the chosen ones and are a bearer of cosmic knowledge."

I felt like Spider-Man listening to Uncle Ben.

The witch from the play park concluded by suggesting that I should study lore surrounding the number 11, that I might be pleasantly surprised. The Gabriela Wiener who'd just walked up a steep hill pushing an empty stroller, carrying shopping bags, and somehow maneuvering to both wipe the sweat from her brow and keep a bawling Lena from slipping through her hands felt everything slide into place. If this wasn't divine ordainment, why the hell would she be heading back home to make fried chicken for her family? There had to be some transcendental explanation for the fact that she hadn't had sex for a month.

Her whole life she had believed she was special, for better or for worse. Gabriela had abandoned her intellect and her intellect had abandoned her. She was exhausted and ready to believe that she was an alien or, at the very least, an alien's messenger.

3

When I got home from the park, I ran to the computer to type in "11" while Lena cried inconsolably in the background. Like the code from *The Matrix*, thousands of testimonies of people suffering the same numerical harassment cascaded down the screen. Knowing that I shared "my secret" with millions of other visionaries infuriated me. Did there have to be so many chosen ones?

On the internet, a guru of the number 11—Solara, a robust blond woman who wears pink tunics and red scarves and organizes meetings in "energetic" places such as Cusco—corroborated what the witch had said. The number 11, I read, surfaces during times of elevated consciousness, and has a powerful effect on those who see it. It's called a "memory trigger" because it activates our cellular memory banks more intensely and makes us feel something stirring deep inside us, as though we were suddenly remembering something we'd forgotten centuries ago.

In short, the number 11 lives in all things, like a cosmic reminder that universal consciousness was once undivided. The mission of us select disciples of the number 11 is to recall this time and to communicate it to the rest of humanity.

But what kind of idiot sent this many invitations to a party that was supposed to be so exclusive?

4

Four years had gone by since my era of full-time motherhood and cosmic park revelations when I realized that something unusual was about to happen—something that only happens once every millennium: 11/11/11, the eleventh of the eleventh of the eleventh. By then I'd stopped being a housewife and had returned to journalism, although I wasn't exactly working for my dream publication. I'd become the managing editor of a magazine aimed at men who still masturbate over buxom women printed on paper. Every month I had to interview the silicone-enhancee of the moment and ask her if she enjoyed anal sex. As much as the idea amused me, it wasn't a job I could talk to my mother or my snobbier friends about. I liked to imagine myself as a feminist agent behind enemy lines, but the truth is that I was a mercenary for the most vulgar of masculine presses.

When I see photos and videos from back when I used to have interstellar meetings in parks, I hardly recognize myself in those floaty outfits stained with breast milk, that wonky fringe I'd trimmed myself, and that idiotic smile. But even though I'd returned to the productive fold, even though reason had triumphed in my life, since then the number 11 had been tapping on my shoulder with increasing insistence.

And now 11/11/11 was around the corner. Even Jaime, who doesn't believe in anything, reminded me to buy a lottery ticket just in case.

In Spain, one of the biggest lotteries is known as "la ONCE" ("once" being "eleven" in Spanish) and that year—of course—it had launched a special lottery with a prize of 11 million euros. Predictably, I waited until the last day. At the entrance to the Boquería market I bought ticket number 55860 from a man in a wheelchair. The total of the digits didn't even give a multiple of 11, but it was the only one left. I put it in my wallet and waited.

Interestingly, according to the Chinese horoscope, 2011 was the year of the rabbit, my year.

5

In the graphic novel I was reading at the time, Alison Bechdel's *Are You My Mother?*, the writer-protagonist analyzes one of her dreams, which features the number 11: "'There is nothing arbitrary or undetermined in the psychic life,' Freud insists. Numbers in particular. Eleven is the first number that can't be counted on two human hands. It goes beyond, transgresses, and for that reason has an association with sin." For the witch in the park it was a divine number, but for the psychoanalyst it was cursed. Its sin, according to Freud, lies in its incompleteness. It sits between 10, the number of human perspective, and 12, the number of cosmic perspective. After Judas's betrayal, the number of apostles was reduced to 11.

Eleven is a number bitterly related to the attacks and natural disasters that have occurred in recent years. The internet is plagued with theories that deconstruct every aspect of the attack on the World Trade Center, from the date (9/11) and the towers (they formed the shape of a number 11), to one of the flight's numbers (11), the number of cabin crew on one of the flights (11), the death toll in that plane (92: 9 + 2 = 11), and the United States emergency number (911 = 9/11), which millions of people called that day. It took eleven years to build the towers.

The same happened with the attacks of March 11, 2004 in Madrid. The death toll was 191: 1 + 9 + 1 = 11; and the date, 1 + 1 + 3 + 2 + 0 + 0 + 4 = 11. Eleven everywhere.

Remembrance Day in the United Kingdom is 11/11. And even the Fourth of July in the United States contains an 11: 4 + 7 = 11. The earthquake that caused the nuclear disaster in Fukushima happened on March 11, 2011. The Oslo attacks happened on July 22, 2011. Oh, and Kennedy died on 11/22.

These macabre "discoveries" had been spreading around the internet for years on sites such as the one run by Uri Geller, a mentalist who bends spoons, and Rik Clay, a young geek who committed suicide shortly after being interviewed on the radio about his findings (although some of his followers still think he was the victim of a government conspiracy and was assassinated so he wouldn't keep talking). All these internet visionaries predicted that the apocalypse would take place on 11/11/11. A year later, according to the Mayans, we'd burn for good.

Why me? Why does the cursed number pursue me? Am I a tool of the Devil? I'm embarrassed to admit this, but I think I caused the earthquake in Chile in 2010. And the earthquake in Pisco, Peru. I was also responsible for David Bowie sticking a sweet in his eye, Morrissey getting drunk on a plane and never making it to the Benicàssim festival, and Keith Richards falling out of a coconut tree. Whenever I travel somewhere, whenever I decide to go to a concert, something is either canceled or destroyed. I used to think it was just bad luck, but when your bad luck casts a shadow on thousands of other people it starts getting to you. Pythagoras was the first to theorize that the universe as a whole emits sounds, much like an enormous piano where any act is akin to hitting a key. Even the faintest sound has some sort of repercussion somewhere in the universe. The flapping of a butterfly's wings can cause a tsunami, no?

One of many films about the mystery of 11/11/11 came out in 2011. It was filmed in Barcelona, where I lived, coincidentally, until 2011. It's about a writer who loses his wife and son. When he moves to Barcelona he begins to notice the insistent appearance of the number 11. He eventually discovers that the number is a message sent to a series of people by guardian angels who, for years, have been trying to warn the world of the imminent opening, which will occur on 11/11/11, of a portal leading to a dimension out of which, so they say, something unimaginable will emerge. As I watched the movie I recognized the setting of one of its scenes—it was Labyrinth Park, a place where we used to play hide-and-seek with Lena, except in the film it's not mommy chasing you, it's a dark and terrible monster.

6

At some point during 2011, I noticed that the writer Iván Thays made "11:11" his Facebook status. Thays was the only person I knew who publicly admitted to seeing the number 11 everywhere, and for some reason it seemed to me that the fact that a cultured man believed in something so ridiculous legitimized my own absurdity. Iván told me he'd been seeing the number since he was nine or ten. He was a real veteran. He even remembered the exact moment he saw it for the first time. It happened over the summer holidays. He was about to go outside to play with his cousin. He looked at the time, it was 11:11 a.m., and thought: I'm going to be seeing that forever. And he did. In one of his literature workshops, he read a student's story in which the protagonist gets up at 11:11 a.m. every day. That's how Thays knew he was not alone. He sees the number 11 on tickets, license plates, and cards. He sees it most often, he says, when he's feeling particularly spiritual or is in need of guidance. And even if it happens all the time, it always takes him by surprise. Thays also told me that the number 11 lends itself easily to a bunch of conspiracy crap. Instead of listening to this nonsense, he tells me, you should find out what the number means to you. For him it's a reminder. When it happens, he stops what he is doing, has a talk with himself because he feels something inside him is asking to be heard, and says a prayer. I think again about the witch in the park and ask him whether we 11'ers have a collective mission in this world.

"No way," he replies. "It's a very personal thing. Each person, whether they see number 11 or not, has a mission in this world."

I joined the Facebook group "11:11," which Thays belonged to. It wasn't very active and it was administrated by Hachinowi Brown, a Peruvian girl who once tried to organize a members' outing that no one attended.

I emailed another writer: the Spanish physicist, poet, and novelist Agustín Fernández Mallo, a man who turned Nocilla (think Nutella) into a literary project emblematic of a generation of Spanish writers. I asked whether in that brain of his—all structured knowledge, empirical evidence, and scientific logic—there was any room at all for the number 11; whether an accumulation of delirious ideas that people shared on the internet could make scientists smash their test tubes and look to the skies for signs of an impending apocalypse. His answer was resolute: all of this is entirely unfounded.

"We're talking about dramatic, often paranoid interpretations of a social construct: numbers. This is a mental abstraction, fodder for the foolish, a mishmash of pseudoscientific concepts," he added. "It's like believing in the apparitions of Our Lady of Lourdes," he said, to settle the matter. "You see 11:11 everywhere because you want to, that's all. It could happen just as easily with 19:64. It's an a posteriori thought. Don't be so gullible, Gaby!"

I finished reading his email and looked at the clock expecting to see the number 11:11, but it was 10:35.

7

I was always terrible at math. Maybe that's why 11 seems so esoteric to me, because I don't understand anything about numbers. I'm not prepared to be likened to someone who believes in the apparitions of the Virgin of Lourdes, but I didn't seek out the number 11; it sought me. Things that happened in 2011: on 2/11/2011 the Egyptian revolution won and Mubarak stepped down as President; on 4/11/2011 there was a metro attack in Minsk and 11 people died; and on 5/11/2011 a strong earthquake struck Lorca. In 2011, Berlusconi resigned, and both Gaddafi and Osama bin Laden died.

I decided to conduct a mathematical experiment with that number that had catapulted the suicidal Rik Clay and Uri Geller to internet fame. I could surely find a meaningful 11 in my personal history. I started out by adding up the letters in my full name and got 19. I then added up the numerals in my date of birth and got 30. I kept trying, but I didn't get any elevens unless I tweaked things a little. The same has happened with most of the results you find all over the internet. Once they've had some luck with some of their discoveries, investigators tend to force adverse reality to fit their theories. This phenomenon is called "information bias," the tendency to favor the facts that confirm one's own beliefs, to gather data selectively, and to interpret it partially and tendentiously.

I was heartbroken. How would you react if your beliefs were taken as fabrications, if your life, your name and your prestige were seriously muddied? You'd think this would make for a good suicide motive, but us 11'ers have never been much for logical inclinations.

8

Spiritualists are more fun than psychologists because they talk instead of making you do the talking. I'm mesmerized when they talk about me, even if it's mere speculation and lies. Two of my friends are my secret bridges to the world of all things spiritual and magic, though I tend to deny this in public. My spirituality has never come out of the closet. I don't tell anyone that I always carry around a blue stone a friend gave me to help me out of a case of writer's block. And that before she gave it to me she ran it all over my body in a ritual with candles and salt spread on the floor. Or that underneath my bed there are five-cent coins I have to be careful not to sweep up if I don't want us to go broke. We've all carried out one operation of religious syncretism or another at our domestic altars.

Is there any difference between the doors of consciousness the number 11 opens up and the mystic rapture of the Kabbalah, yoga, Sufism, tarot, Tantra, and psychomagic? All those practices also talk about energy, change, synchronicity, symbolic correspondences, cosmic intuition, angels, mandalas, candles, and karma.

Occasionally, the writer and film director Alejandro Jodorowsky will tweet things like: "11:11=22. It's a divine number. It's the number 11 looking at itself in a mirror. Your divine double is seeking you out. It's time to open your ego to your essential Being."

Do I believe in all this? What I definitely don't believe in are coincidences. Too many strange things have happened for me to put them down to statistics, chance, and déjà vu. So I carry around my lapis lazuli just in case the esoterics turn out to be as right as they are mad.

With another friend, a prenatal yoga teacher, I chat online about psychoanalysis and astrology. I get a nice buzz off her delirious readings of my personality and my future. I know few women over thirty who don't proudly self-define as "spiritual." I'm still in the closet, but I like to think it's because I've got a life.

9

My parents never sang "Jesus loves me" lullabies at bedtime, they never had me baptized, they never made me kneel down in a church, they never hung up a crucifix in the house. It was only my grandmothers who tried to ensure my sister and I wouldn't be taken by the devil. Every morning, at 11, my grandmothers would stop what they were doing, switch off our cartoons, and tune in to a particular radio station. Sitting with bowed heads, they would slip their rosary beads between their fingers with their eyes closed while the beautiful Schubert aria gradually filled all corners of the room. "Hail Mary, full of grace. Our Lord is with thee. Blessed art thou among women, and blessed is the fruit of thy womb, Jesus. Holy Mary, Mother of God, pray for us sinners, now and at the hour of our death. Amen." And I prayed in secret just in case my grandmothers were right and God did exist. Much like I now carry a little stone in my purse.

I met Gisella, a strange and introverted young woman who was studying Education, when I was a college student. I have no idea how we became friends. I think by then I had stopped caring what others thought and was trying to only hang out with the people who seemed genuinely happy and fun. She wanted to be a nun.

I was trying to cool my insufferable ego. I remember our long discussions about God, and all the Catholic youth meetings we went to together to see if Catholicism was my path. Catholicism gave way to carnality not long afterward, and I moved away from God for a long, long time.

My mother, on the other hand, abandoned politics and stopped being an atheist. Now, every time something important happens in my life, she tells me it's the angels protecting me. She says she sees me even though I'm far away, she feels me, she senses what's happening to me. She calls herself a "Mochica priestess." My maternal family come from the Mochica people's lands. Their supreme God was "the decapitator," and they practiced human sacrifice.

When I'm desperate, I sometimes go to the sea to pray for things to happen, or to never happen. Clearly, my dealings with God have always been pretty flighty.

10

Unlike September 21, 2012—the date for the end of the world according to the Mayan people—11/11/11 didn't herald catastrophic prophecies. For Solara, shaman of the number 11, the gates to the otherworld open at long last. We would all enter into synchronicity and the planet's consciousness would change, as if someone had pressed a giant reset button. Not only had ceremonies and meditation rituals been planned around the world: in some countries like Switzerland, thousands of couples would get married and hundreds of babies would be born by planned cesarean to absorb the energy of that day.

"We'll come together in a single heart, soul, and thought in order to unite ourselves with the wisest and most ancient cultures," said the Institute of Holistic Investigation in France.

In Argentina, at the foot of Mount Uritorco, Matías de Stefano, a young man who claims to be the reincarnation of a citizen of Atlantis, managed to bring together twelve thousand people hoping to be enlightened.

In Egypt, meanwhile, the military junta managed to sabotage the ceremony that thousands of "human angels" were going to perform at the Great Pyramid of Giza to gather sacred energy and thereby create a shield between Earth and the cosmos. They were accused of being Satanists. The outraged esoterics warned that without this protection, everything would come to an end on 12/12/12.

11

On 11/11/11, a Friday, I awoke to the sun shining in Barcelona. I opened my eyes, checked my email on my iPhone. I'd been sent a hotel reservation number and my AVE train ticket to Madrid. I was to start work on Monday. In the midst of the Spanish economic crisis, I'd been offered a good job at a women's magazine with a much better salary and, more exciting, the possibility of replenishing my collection of perfumes and creams. It wasn't bad. My friends, half of them unemployed, couldn't believe it. I'd secretly desired it, and now it was happening. Information bias?

On 11/11/11 I dressed in black, as always. It was my last day at the bizarre fake tits publication for men. Soon I'd be in charge of a magazine for women who like dresses and cosmetics. I was leaving the city I'd lived in for the past eight years. One door was closing and another was opening. Before leaving for the office, I decided to wait until it was 11:11 a.m. I wanted to be with Jaime.

At 11:11 on 11/11/11, I looked at the clock on my phone and ran with it in my hand down the long corridor of our apartment. I managed to drag Jaime away from the computer and into our bedroom. I asked him if we could close our eyes and pray for our life in Madrid, as if we were counting beads on an alternative rosary. Then we went out into the brightness of the balcony.

Shortly after 11:11 on 11/11/11, I wrote an email saying goodbye to my colleagues. It read: "The last few nights I've gone to bed early and curled up in a fetal position trying to pretend it's not me who has to face a new life all over again. Being scared shitless is important, I know. But today I woke up feeling braver, and at 11:11, I took a selfie with a clock in the background like an idiot. So here I am, a hypersensitive New Age loser, ready to say goodbye." Irony, absurdity, humor. And truth.

At 3 p.m. on 11/11/11, I left my old office and walked along Paseo San Juan, feeling like someone ephemerally liberated. I don't know what I ate. Or where. I picked Lena up from school and helped her write goodbye letters to her friends.

At 7:19 p.m. on 11/11/11, I got an email from Christian Basilis, editor-in-chief of the magazine *Orsai*, with whom I'd talked about the number 11 weeks before. He asked me what my columns in *Orsai* would be about during 2012, and I replied that they'd be about the end of the world. He was pleased.

I told him I was moving to Madrid. He told me he was moving back to Argentina. We were both surprised, we wished each other well.

That day, Iván Thays took part in a ceremony on a beach. It was very inspirational, but ultimately lacked consequence. Hachinowi went camping by a lake with her husband and her dog, Vincent. At 11:11, they meditated and absorbed the positive energy of the place. Nothing much changed. As for the lottery ticket, that day I lost a million euros because the winning number was 56850 and mine was 55860. I was really close (6 + 5 = 11).

ON MOTHERLINESS

THEY LOOK SO SMALL, so portable, that you want to pack them into a suitcase just to see if they'll fit. These are impulses that over time a parent learns to repress. You have to monitor actions and reactions like a hawk to ensure you don't cause the fledgling creature any permanent damage. That's what this whole experiment is about. I used to think that when you become a mother you lose your stupidity all of a sudden; that some mechanism is mysteriously set in motion, and the autopilot on a trip to maturity gets automatically switched on. There is no such thing. I've taken many an honest look at myself in the mirror of motherhood. Sometimes you like what you see, sometimes you don't.

One day, sooner rather than later, you'll be disarmed by your child's ability to laugh, the unflappability with which they take on the challenge of being your child. And you'll see that there was nothing much to worry about. The healthiest thing is not to allow your child to think for one minute that you're better than you actually are. Your best gift will be to save your child this one disappointment, probably the first of their life, because there'll be plenty more to come.

Of course, you shouldn't make them believe that you're worse than you are, either. That would be an even bigger mistake, and could cost you their weight in therapy.

Sooner or later they will realize you're not postmodern, just an imbecile; that you're not funny, just careless and irresponsible; that you're not strict, just bitter; that you're not free-spirited, just a slacker; and that you're not their friend, just their mother. But that will be further down the line. In the meantime, enjoy:

"Mom."

"What is it?"

"Come here."

"What's wrong?"

"I'll tell you when you get here."

"Okay, I'm here, what do you want?"

"Got you!!!!"

Last night we took her to a café. With this cold weather, you can't be out in the parks. Also, let's face it, parks are boring. Since the smoking ban was put in effect, cafés have become the favorite place for mothers and children: a smoke-free space where mothers can rest their chin in their hand while the nice waitresses entertain the children with that magic thing that fills glasses with bubbly liquid. It was supposed to be a wild night out for us parents. She was going to have a sleepover at her cool uncle's house. But when it was time for mommy to take her to her cool uncle's house, the girl started talking like Tarzan. "Me sleep with Mommy." "Home mommy," "mommy home." And before I knew it, we were all back at home and in bed. Increasingly insomniac, increasingly lucid. As we count sheep, I swear I can hear Dr. Estivill and Dr. González bickering in the background about their respective, diametrically opposed methods for putting children to bed.

*

"I'm not going anywhere, I'm right next door. See? There's nothing in your closet."

"Mom, I want to be with Mom. Mom, Mom, Mom. You're so pretty, so intelligent. Mom, cuddle me to sleep." She says it all with an irresistible smile, dewy eyes, and outstretched arms, and you have no choice but to get under the covers with her and give her everything she's asking for, which is simultaneously not much and all you have, all you are, and all you will be. "Night, Mom."

I made a pact with her: I would read her a story, then I would leave and she would read the next one by herself. She agreed to it. I couldn't believe it. She found the experiment interesting. I would give her a little kiss and disappear. It was two weeks of heaven. But by the third week she hadn't just annulled our pact, she'd regressed. I was back to reading her three stories, half of them in Catalan, by the way, while she corrected my absurd pronunciation. Then she decided I wasn't going anywhere, not after three stories, not after song number eight, not now, not ever. Every night I curled up in a fetal position, my back breaking on the edge of her cute little Ikea bed.

I sleep, I sleep not, I sleep, I sleep not, I sleep, I sleep not, I sleep, I sleep not, I sleep, I sleep not, I sleep, I sleep not, I sleep, I sleep not . . . I pluck the petals off my dreams.

Basically, I believe that youth is a drug. Children are always in a state of altered consciousness. Which is to be expected, since they've been in this world for so little time. They're like annoying tourists: excited about everything and leaving their plastic cups everywhere. Bedtime doesn't even register with them. Today I read her the story of *The Princess and the Pea*. I had to read it five times because every time we reached the end she started crying if I didn't start over. The fifth time I read it I was interrupted by my own heavy breathing and snores. If I started to nod off I'd hear a distant "Mommmmm," a voice that came from far-off lands, and I dragged myself up to the surface, trying to climb out of that bottomless pit of sleep. I had no idea what I was reading, but it was my voice, of course it had to be my voice, and the next thing I know I'm wide awake and telling Lena about the King of Spain's brother-in-law's embezzlement conviction. That's when I knew it was over. Increasingly insomniac, increasingly lucid.

Today I tried to explain to my daughter what "dead time" is: "There are moments when we do absolutely nothing, and life is full of those, my love." She replied, "Who killed it?" I was going to say that what matters is not who killed it but how it was killed—but by then she'd already switched on the TV.

"Can't you see I look ridiculous?" she exclaims, her eyes burning with indignation, as if she weren't three feet tall. She knows nothing about life, and despite this, or maybe because of it, I can only take her seriously. Defeated, I remove the scarf from her fragile little neck before we head out to school.

When Dad (not just any dad: he does his equal share of housework and tends to take on the most thankless tasks) goes away, Mom (not just any mom, but me) is concerned about one thing only: how to fill the canvas of the twenty-four hours she will spend alone with her daughter.

The solution always tends to be the same: call a friend, reel them in under the pretense of grabbing a beer, and then end up in a play park next to the swings. It's a good strategy to get away from other parents who are as obnoxious as you are.

But today, as is increasingly the case, I can't trick anyone into coming. That's why, as I head out of work to pick her up, I mentally prepare myself for the impending—fear? responsibility? boredom?

I wait for her at the gate and there she is, beautiful, her eyes burning with excitement when she sees me. She hands me a chorizo. That's right, a damn chorizo she's made herself on her trip to a farm. "In one minute and a half there will be a downpour," she declares very seriously. But when we walk in search of our afternoon snack, the sky clears and I give in to the joy of having her all to myself.

My husband and I kiss on the lips. My daughter and I kiss on the lips. My husband and my daughter kiss on the lips. And what separates these kisses has little to do with the crazed views of hand-wringing puritans. Some people warn of the dangers of the "early eroticization" of children. If it's all right for your father to kiss you on the mouth, then maybe it's all right for anyone to kiss you on the lips. I'd like to counter this with a warning on the dangers of expressing love not from a place of affection, but from a place of mistrust. It's true that evil exists—the demented, the imbeciles, the sexists, the racists, and the pedophile priests—but I want to believe in our ability to discern, in our intelligence and ability to care without repressing ourselves. And I think about those parents who blush at kissing scenes; who avoid "the talk," who find it more natural to slap their children than to kiss them. It's true that we all have our own way of expressing ourselves, our habits, and our misgivings. And that's all right. But, if I may, I'm going to place myself firmly on the side of those parents who have not allowed themselves to be intimidated and who are able to admit that there's a sensuality—not a sexuality—in their relationship with their pups. For millennia, mothers fed their children by mouth, like birds. Because of that memory, people who love each other bring their lips together. Although we no longer feed the body that way, we feed our souls.

"Why are they so sad?" my daughter asks at the museum in front of *Adam and Eve Expelled from Paradise*. Because they've been expelled from Paradise. Who expelled them? God expelled them. Why did he do it? Because Eve gave Adam a forbidden apple. And who gave it to her? A serpent who was the devil. And why did he give it to Eve and not to Adam? It's an important question. It's *the* question. For a moment, I am stumped. The Book of Genesis may be more far-fetched than *Sleeping Beauty*, but a feminist mother should still be able to answer a question of that caliber. Lena looks at me with her expectant seven-year-old eyes twinkling the way they do every time she works her implacable logic against me.

When she was only two, she stole my pads and, dying of laughter, stuck them on her back like two fragile wings before running off. She had no idea her play wings would one day bear her own blood. Now she's better informed, especially since I was foolish enough to show her a video of a natural birth. Since then she is adamant that she will not have children. I tell her that if having children ever makes any sense to her, the pain will be the least of her problems, but that if she really doesn't want to, she will absolutely be within her rights not to do it. And then I drag her to pro-choice marches or protests against gender violence, and when she gets bored of my proclamations, I remind her of our conversation in the museum in front of the painting. I remind her of the absurd story they've been telling women for generation after generation—a story that casts us as the witches, the ribs, the confused ones, the guilty ones, the weak ones, the mothers of all calamities. That's why, I say to my daughter, we need to tell each other different stories, ones that are truer, fairer, more ours; like the story where we are friends with the serpent and screw Paradise anyway.

We thought one day we'd grow up and forget about the mutilation, but no. It's still there, intact: the moment when the little girl tells her mother, with tears in her eyes, that a little boy told her he might like her if she was "white." The mother kidnaps the boy and leaves him at the bottom of a well. She feeds him just enough to turn him into a famished and deformed creature who can't tell a worm from a stone.

You are not alone. When they insult you, they are insulting a multitude. So let us give thanks for our violence, said the worm in Bolaño's poem, crawling along the horizon of fear and desire. That memory of adversity is an automatic firearm: I read, I think, and I rip out guts. I howl with Bolaño's *Romantic Dogs*, those who are no longer afraid of anything. Anyone who has ever felt marginalized should read that book. To recognize oneself is a fabulous adventure. The long-dispossessed, the gay, the ugly, the sex addicts, the premature ejaculators, the fat women, the ill—with their mouths full of wild and beautiful words that shouldn't be stoppered.

It's interesting to discover how the little monster is still howling from the depths of the well, but by then you're already a long way away from there, as if you possessed the most indestructible spirit, "the most absolute beauty, that which contains all the greatness and misery in the world."

My daughter asks why the boys at school have to hit the girls with their umbrellas. I say to her, "Boys are like that, they like girls, but when they're little they're scared of them and sometimes don't really know how to handle their feelings."

"And that's why they hit me?"

I think it through and say to her, "No, they hit you because they're stupid."

My daughter and I sometimes cross the Paseo del Prado with her bike, and we reach the same corner where, three days ago, the police captured a protester—one of the thousands protesting Rajoy's government—grabbed her by the neck, dragged her, slammed her on the floor, and later arrested her for rioting.

My daughter and I have never been in Ranrapata, where a little girl named Zoraida was killed by a "stray" bullet. Every time I get frustrated, my daughter witnesses my yelling with a fearful look on her face and eyes full of tears. "You're mean!" she yells back at me. We try to defend ourselves from each other, and end up attacking each other.

*

My daughter watches television. The Disney Channel, for example. In 80 percent of the series, the girls are completely idiotic and frivolous. My daughter says to her dad, after he kills a giant mosquito, "my heart is trembling."

My daughter is an intelligent girl, she learns new things every day; she draws portraits of Chinese emperors, she writes three-line novels, and she also just became a fan of Elvis.

Sometimes people ask me if I'm scared of her reading the things that I've published, the things I've "confessed."

I've never confessed anything. There's something perverse in the word "confession." Within it lives the word "guilt." I usually reply that I'm not afraid because I know my daughter knows the value of truth.

I think again about boys hitting girls with their umbrellas. And I say to myself that silly little boys need to be forgiven and taught better, but silly grown-ups simply need to be fought. With everything we've got.

I still remember—with surprising precision considering the rather poor caliber of my memory—the first word I read: "crown." It was when I was looking out of the window of my dad's car, and that first feeling of having extracted meaning from some signs painted on the wall, that revelation, was like discovering fire.

I wasn't there when my daughter read her first word ("table"), but each day she and I laugh at the adventures of Captain Arsenio, we fly with Watanabe's painted bird, we run around with Pippi Longstocking, or we disappear under Harry Potter's invisibility cloak. It's not always easy. I find it very hard to make her understand that stories are not just a bedtime toy, I find it hard to peel her away from the TV, I struggle to get her to understand that a book can contain a different story each time we reread it.

But I am optimistic. I want to believe that time and patience will lead her to her own revelation. And I wonder if it will be with words such as *Othello* or *musketeer*—as happened with her father—or with words like *dough* or *herald*—as it happened to me. And sometimes, when I've already read her several pages and I'm tired and she stays awake with the book in her hands, I hear her murmur parts of words. And I can hear her laugh from my room. She laughs like only children can laugh while reading.

One of the first poems from my mythical unpublished poetry collection is titled "Deconstruction of the father." I wrote it based on fifty poems by Raúl Wiener, typewritten and corrected by hand between 1968 and 1972. To say that I wrote it is taking it a bit far. My work constituted exclusively in picking out some of my father's verses from different texts and mixing them up in a sequence like a DJ sampling other people's music. At the mixing desk, the grown-up daughter, now in her thirties, decides to play at her leisure with these words, which somehow feel intimate, her own.

Some people destroy the father, others deconstruct him. The result of that poetic experiment is strange, like hearing versions of José Feliciano in a remix by Trent Reznor.

Some inherit money, others illustrious surnames they don't deserve. I inherited that stack of yellowed documents—a point of departure—poems written on the back of some horrible statistical notebook about hydrocarbon investments by a young and lyrical man who would go on to become a ferocious and committed thinker, filling millions of critical and necessary pages, but who would never publish his poems.

Yesterday, perhaps because I spent a good part of the day watching a series about a women's prison and taking advantage of my mother's regular Sunday phone call (which is always followed by an extremely long email of recommendations and blessings, as is common with mothers of children who have made their nests very far from the nest), I asked her to tell me the story of those days of the ill-fated dictatorship when she was pregnant with me and my dad was a political prisoner. "How strange that I didn't talk about it in my book about pregnancy, don't you think, Mom?"

"Yes, love, especially since you aren't usually one to hold back . . . When I was pregnant with your sister, I ran away from the police in the middle of a national strike. And for most of my pregnancy with you I was paying your dad conjugal visits."

In the photo, my mother and I (my dad is not pictured, but he was home, finally free, wearing his bell-bottoms and sideburns) are giving each other our first doses of uninterrupted love.

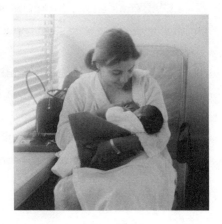

Lena came over to me the other day with a mischievous grin. "Mom, why didn't you tell me we had this book?" she said, handing over *New Ways to Kill Your Mother* by Colm Tóibín. This is it, I thought. I always knew it would happen, I just never imagined it would happen so soon. She's just like me but worse (or better, dammit). Playing along, I explained that the book was an essay on the relationship between writers and their families, not a practical guide. And cursing the warrior movies that she watches every day, I swapped the book for another one more suitable to her six years of age, thinking that would be the end of it. But the next day, Jaime texted me: "I just found *Kill the Father* by Amélie Nothomb under Lena's bed. We are in REAL danger. I'm telling you, she's plotting something." I laughed, then wondered if she might really want to take us out. "She hates us and is planning her revenge," Jaime joked.

That same night, our daughter called out to us in tears—something she hadn't done since she was a baby—and said that she was afraid of dying. She said all she could think about was "nasty things" and that she was scared of not being able to get them out of her head. We cuddled her for hours while she held on to us very tight. It was the first time she'd spoken to us about death, and it was terrifying.

My little girl is growing up and, like all children do, is traversing a developmental phase that consists of both fearing and desiring the death of her parents, whose absence at her age would be an absolute. Wanting to eliminate us is a desire that will inevitably recur, although our murder, I hope, will remain a symbolic fantasy.

FROM THIS SIDE
AND FROM THAT SIDE

WE ARE FOG PEOPLE. Every day the fog paws like a cat at our hearts. We are born and grow up to the broken promises of both sun and rain; that's why we are more grateful than anyone for rays of light and the slightest raindrops. The weather, for us, never makes conversation easier.

We are street people. Nomadic by nature. We are the grandchildren of poor, adventurous strangers. Our living radicalizes their legacy. They left chaos behind only so that we could recreate it. Our chaos is where our vitality resides, it's what makes us untamable. We suffer, buy, sell, eat, observe, flee, and love in the streets, fluorescent. We burn the asphalt. We leave often. And sometimes we even come back.

We are sea people. Our ship is a beached whale circled by vultures. For us, everything rots and everything comes back to life beside the waves. We dig deep pits at the edge of things. We prefer our bottles with no messages in them.

We are night people. People of long-since shuttered bars and drugs and alcohol-induced visions. Of secret maps, disenchantment, and staircases leading nowhere. Our poets write the most beautiful words in the world. And then they die.

We are shit people. Sometimes we are. There is no other explanation for all this hatred and rubble. We build our homes not to live in them, but to survive in spite of them. This is out city, perhaps our only chance on earth. But we are young and implausible. We have the fog, the street, the sea, and the night in common. Not shit.

We bring a beach towel and even a ball. We're so behind the times. We'd forgotten that La Herradura no longer has a beach; the turncoat sea swept away all the sand that had been brought in by the truckload under orders of the first woman elected mayor of Lima. La Herradura no longer has a shore or its chromatic yachts. The sea, smelling of all the dead bodies in the history of the world, makes us want to drink.

The old waiter who served our ceviche tilted our plates, swirling the salty, spicy *leche de tigre*. He entertained us with stories I wish I had written: The "big fish" had moved out of those white rusty buildings near La Herradura tunnel, so the old man had started carrying *jaleas*—fried seafood platters—all the way to their new, carpeted apartments, where their mistresses also awaited, wrapped in white towels and with a puff of white powder on their nostrils. Old-time beach ostentatiousness metamorphosed, unhinged. Can there be anything more inspiring than this perfect decadence? Sometimes I swear I'm not seeing it but inventing it.

Faced with the desolate landscape, Rocío, a foreigner after all, said she'd never seen seagulls black as crows, and everything seemed to her a sign of the end of the world. Lena, a child after all, joyfully threw pebbles onto pebbles. Jaime, a poet after all, spoke about invisible apartments and the cars that drive in and out of nothingness. And I suggested we head for the decrepit white buildings and examine the magnitude of their abandonment.

As I walk across the main square in Lima's Barranco district, I'm confronted with an image that I'd never seen before, though it may have been there all along, hiding behind the foliage: a group of sculptures of the most recent presidents of Peru exhibited by a restaurant as a part of its kitsch garden décor. Whether they're a highly suspect political manifesto or a bizarre marketing strategy, they're definitely a punch to the gut. Which isn't really what you want at a restaurant. They're all there: Belaúnde, Fujimori, Toledo, and García—the cream of the crop of our recent political freak show. How much disillusionment those names contain, and how much theft. Someone, or maybe all of us thirty million Peruvians, forgot to fling them into the fire of oblivion. We're still letting them dine at the next table over. We even pick up their bill.

From up close, they look like a group of friends carousing around the table, with their papier-mâché brains and their wrinkly smiles. But when I take a few steps back, they look cornered, conservative, corrupt, and failed. I back up more, and peer through the metal bars of the restaurant's façade. They look lonely and absurd.

From the plane, the city meets the sunrise like any other, its periphery scintillatingly alight. As we descend, the city awakes and unfurls in my memory. The cafes, terraces, and bars. The promenades and the taximeters. Another way of doing politics, another form of corruption, other kinds of propaganda. And the pulse of its everydayness, which I've learned to recognize over years. The peace of its bars and cinemas. I've gotten to know this other city well, and when I step off the plane I feel, in a way, as though I were coming home. The blue sky, the bright white and perfectly delineated clouds.

I recognize the horizontality of its paths and the democracy of its metro, where social classes are temporarily abolished. People's faces seem familiar. So does the violence of their language and their brutal sympathy for all things. For a second of civic schizophrenia, I feel foggy with guilt at the thousands of miles that separate me from Lima. I live in a European capital, but instead of feeling cosmopolitan, it feels nostalgically provincial. As I leave the airport—souvenirs of bullfighters and flamenco dancers, Real Madrid T-shirts—I can't help but wonder what I'm doing, returning to a place that is not mine. I fill the taxi with suitcases. A placid journey to the center of the city awaits. "Where are you from?" the driver asks me, but how to convey the concept of Lima's grayness under this foreign sun?

Years ago, when I first arrived in Madrid, I carried with me an inner Lima as an insatiable hunger, out of which sprouted new cities and gaps and habits. I missed the food. I missed a form of relaxation that here feels more like wasting time. I missed the people. But moving to another city is to change the accent of your affections. It took only a few years for Lima to become the journey, and for touching down in Madrid to become the return. I cross this other city without delays. Madrid is not a paragon of civic-mindedness, but after two months in Lima it feels like Stockholm. Here, drivers don't seem bent on running over pedestrians, and there is not a single publicity billboard in sight. No candidate for public office in any municipality would think to try and win votes by plastering their face all over the city. I get home still feeling unsettled, dissonant. Perhaps everything feels strange because Madrid will always be "other." And although I no longer leave my heart in Lima every time I return to Madrid, it remains my beloved, my horrible, my gray city.

Paternal abandonment runs through our culture; it's in our idiosyncrasy and our essence. It wafted through the sails of the conquistadors' ships, which set off from our shores laden with gold; it swelled in the gaze of the mestizo Garcilaso de la Vega, anxious at even the slightest snub from the Spanish court; and now it burns in the literature of Ciro Alegría, Vargas Llosa, Arguedas, and Valdelomar.

Our reality and our fiction meet at the junction of irresponsible paternity. Maybe this history of irresponsible paternity is why mothers, utterly unprotected, have had to play the lead role in the most violent struggles of our past. Like Rosa Cuchillo, the unforgettable character in Óscar Colchado's novel, Peruvian women have had to tirelessly search for their disappeared children in the mass graves of unofficial history, under the indifferent gaze of the state.

I demand a paternity test. How can I share anything with this nation, such a fertile ground for satire? Am I in any way consubstantial to its cronyism, miserable deals, and dim collusions? Does its weakness bear any relation to me? To any of us? I want to say no, and I want to believe that most other Peruvians would, too. And yet, we're all part of its disheartening, pathetic production.

"The palace now has the deep silence of a mausoleum and from there we are governed by a cadaver that breathes," said the great José Watanabe to his Antigone.

Do we need to take to the streets again? This seems like a romantic and useless gesture, like throwing pebbles into stagnant, murky waters. But it's better than cowering in the face of power, for if we do cower, one day we might be confronted, as Antigone was, with guilt—"a face that tortures and shames."

They came looking for my father late at night, and the next time I saw him he was on the TV. He was there in the background, on the Uchuraccay hillside. I was excited to see my dad on television for the first time, but what I remember most vividly are the plastic bags. They contained journalists, like my father, except that they were dead.

It was not unusual to come across photographs of dead bodies during the 1980s in Peru. I was obsessed with dead bodies, especially those that came in black plastic bags. I remember the photos of an entire family murdered by Sendero Luminoso particularly well. The front cover of *Caretas* featured the tortured bodies of a family that lay strewn across their garden; the signs around their necks read, in their own blood, "back-stabbing swine." I wondered if that would happen to us.

Caught in the midst of the cross fire, my parents often had to explain these kinds of photos to us—painful and, I realize now, shameful moments for them. If my mom and dad were a bit late coming back from work, I started to cry, thinking they were dead. I would snuggle up holding their pajamas to breathe in their smell, feeling paralyzed with fear of the monster that had stuffed my parents in black plastic bags.

While it lurked in the shadows, we all feared this monster like nothing else. But one day, we switched on the light and all we saw was a chubby man clinging to his own myth.

A civil war is a complex phenomenon, but a monster is just a monster.

Those of us who have seen it up close know it nestles and eats away at you. The worst thing about it is not its ferocity, but its persistence. Those of us who have seen it from up close know what it is to breathe a sigh of relief when it seems to be burning itself out. We know the optimistic twinkle in people's eyes and the hopeful smiles. But it always returns, telling us that hard as we might try, we will never, ever be able to escape. If there's anything I've learned in all these years, it's that it plays with you, as if it had a mind of its own, as if it were more than the sum of its infected parts.

This illness tries to subjugate your will, bring you to your knees. One day you wake up and find it has infected a relative, a friend, and your boss—along with an endless number of collateral victims. At first you yell and protest, and then you try to expose the illness's filthy underside to the light.

But still it persists. In the end it leaves a sediment of sorrow in the soul.

Corruption pollutes indiscriminately, killing hope and starving those who hunger for justice.

I have to give you all bad news: you are all *cholos*. Seriously, you are all straight-up cholos.

Let me explain: It was the Lima of the 1980s, very Arnold and Willis, and it was a private school where kids played at building hierarchies by comparing the shades of their skin. Little five-year-old despots preaching the gospel of our society: "a little less black means a little less cholo." I was one of the afflicted—my skin was on the darker end of the color spectrum we used to differentiate amongst ourselves—and therefore grew up believing my classmates were white, my sister was white, my girlfriends were white, and my bosses were white.

But, as I finally realized one day, not a single one of them is white; they are all varying shades of cholo. In Peru, everyone is a cholo. The news anchor is chola, for example. The soap opera actresses are extremely cholas, including the blond ones. The criollo writers, particularly those "non-Andean" ones, are cholos. There are tough cholos, big cholos, fat cholos, rich cholas, and swanky cholas. Even the first lady is a Chinese chola. Here in our castle of cholitude, we might as well try to make sense of things together.

I came to Spain because I was told that my destiny awaited here, in this so-called Europe. The crisis was supposedly "affecting" Europe, but Spain wasn't just "affected," it was a wasteland. Two of my best friends left. One of them went back to Lima and the other one left for Miami, which is basically the same thing. For the first time in decades, emigration was greater than immigration.

I also migrated—but from Barcelona to Madrid. It was a survival handbook move. In desolate Madrid, sometimes I imagined that only Mario Vargas Llosa and I were left behind. I used to be considered unusual for being Peruvian and not working as a maid. Then I began to stick out because I had a job, full stop. Some people even thought I was German.

When exactly was it that Spain fell apart?

Near my apartment there's a Peruvian restaurant, La Lupita, famous for serving the best *pollo a la brasa* in the world amidst crying children, cumbia at full blast, and botched electrical wiring. Some days I go there just so that when I leave, I feel like I'm in the First World again.

When I arrived in 2003, Spain still had money to burn and was a place you felt glad to live in. Because it was a newly rich country (which in its day had survived a bleak civil war, a long dictatorship, and a debatable transition), it flaunted its shiny new membership to the club of the owners of the world. I didn't get the memo, though. I had just arrived and was too busy surviving. I was an individual in crisis when everything around me was glorying in the abundance, and by the time I was prepared to reap my share, the crisis had hit everyone else.

But the Spanish government is one thing and the Spaniards are something else entirely. Gradually, Spain changed the rules of its game, and then faced off against the Spaniards.

"Beware, Spain, of your own Spain," wrote César Vallejo. "Beware of the victim in spite of himself, of the hangman in spite of himself and of the uncommitted in spite of himself! Beware of the new potentates! Beware of the one who eats your corpses, of the one who devours your living dead! Beware of your heroes! Beware of the future!"

How right Vallejo was. It's not that poets are seers; it's that countries are blind.

Beware, Peru, of your own Peru.

In order to be decidedly un-European: never be on time, never plan ahead, care very little about the holidays, have a dismal savings account, and never look effortlessly elegant. Or, alternatively, pack turtlenecks while everyone is waxing and trying on new bikinis. Live halfway around the world for months, and return once a year to the corner from which you came, precisely for its cold season.

"I'm afraid," sings Carlos Gardel, "of encountering my past." For those of us who left Peru, the past isn't behind us, it's a horizon on the other side of the ocean. The stars, as mocking and indifferent as they are in Gardel's tango, witness our return. In real life nobody cares we're back, either, except for a handful of people who gave birth to us, watched us grow, watched us leave, and every so often welcome us back. There are no old cardboard boxes to be opened on the other side, because by now we've even taken our most yellowed books and thrown out our last high school notebooks. There are new babies and fewer friendships. We curse the weather and the sky. We take our children to see their roots, and we're once again cradled by the tender madness of our parents.

People always feel the urge to revisit their first love. I, especially, am compelled to do so. After all, I was brought up to be argumentative, and my first love, my country, makes for a good sparring partner.

Regardless, there is no turning back from Operation: Return Home, nor from this trembling emotion.

A WEEKEND WITH MY OWN DEATH

WE ALL HAVE TOMBS from which we travel. To reach mine, I hitch a ride with some strangers to a place in the Catalan Coastal Range. I'll be spending the weekend taking part in a workshop called "Live Your Death." The main act will be to relate my death in the first person, without really dying—I hope. The workshop's brochure makes it sound as though we're about to go through a near-death experience: watch the film of your life, glimpse the light at the end of the tunnel, have out-of-body experiences, and see languid little men calling us affectionately from the threshold where it all ends. It's also possible, I think, that I'll be put on a plane headed for an island where I'll be abducted and eventually indoctrinated into some weird cult. In the meantime, I'm getting to know some of my fellow passengers.

"Did we meet at 'Recycling Ourselves'?" asks the man.

"No, at 'My Place in the Universe.'"

"Oh, yeah . . . So did you find it?"

"I guess not."

"What you need is a clear objective," he says, ignoring her obvious discomfort. The man, despite all the money he's spent on self-help workshops, seems not to have grasped certain basic principles. For example, never greet someone by asking her if she's figured out what to do with her shitty life yet. I can think of various things to say to them both to solve their problems and earn myself some cash. He could try closing his mouth every now and then, and she could tell guys who think they know more about her than she does to fuck off.

"Well, girls, are you ready?" This is the man's second time at the death workshop, and he fancies himself an expert.

"You have to take your clothes off. We're all gonna get butt naked, yes, siree."

The woman and I look at each other. The man turns to face me:

"You must have good lungs because you're from down south. You're going to need them. I don't want to give too much away, but they're going to grab you by the hair and drown you a bit."

Even though it's clear he's messing with us, the woman—who tells us her brother persuaded her to come "after the workshop helped him leave his horrible girlfriend and terrible job"—looks shocked.

"Hey, uncross your legs or you'll stop your feminine energy from flowing!" he tells me.

We're nearly there.

The workshop center is a big house in the hills. It's surrounded by trees, has a huge swimming pool overlooking the Mediterranean, and currently houses several different existential workshops. At the front desk, next to the herb tea table, I pay the bill feeling a bit dirty, as if I were paying for drugs. The concept that luxury is a necessary precursor to emotional health seems a flawed one.

I settle into my room, put my four changes of comfortable clothes in the wardrobe, my toiletries in the bathroom, and, what the hell, go out to socialize. Apparently, one of the aims of the workshop is to expose one's true self to others, something normal people usually only do after four drinks. A girl sits down next to me.

"Death?"

"Yes," I say. "You?"

"Same. The word 'death' is already starting to seem a little less scary, don't you think?"

"Uh . . . I guess." I ask her who the women dressed in white are.

"They're with 'Apologize to Your Mother.' Is it your first time?"

I tell her it is.

"I'm so jealous! It's going to be one of the most important experiences of your life. This is my fourth time."

People tend to come multiple times, which, depending on how you look at it, is either a very good or a very bad sign. A bell rings and we go into the main room. There are more than thirty of us in 'Live Your Death,' and none of us are wearing shoes. The workshop leader asks us to introduce ourselves and say why we've come. He looks at me and says "You start," so I do:

"My name's Gabriela. I'm Peruvian, but I've been living in Barcelona for eight years. I've come because . . . I'm afraid of death and because I feel disconnected . . . "

I say all this because it's the truth. There are other truths, but we've been asked to keep it brief.

Before coming, we were all asked to sign a confidentiality agreement, which is why I've deliberately changed the name of the workshop and I won't use any proper names, not even the name of the person who led the workshop, a famous Catalonian intellectual. We also had to complete a psychological test, which required that we rank eighteen concepts from best to worst. For example, I ranked blowing up an airplane full of passengers sixteenth, burning a heretic alive seventeenth, and torturing someone last.

One by one the others share their reasons for attending, all of which have to do with finding themselves.

The workshop leader explains that this is not therapy. He says it's an experience that won't heal the ego; it will dissolve it—which is what death ultimately does to us all. This will be a rite of initiation and catharsis that kills the selfish child we all still carry inside, allowing us to find our place in a cosmic, social, and familial framework. He tells us that to fear death is to fear life, and to get over our fear, we must confront the concept of "impermanence."

The workshop will culminate once we have "lovingly discovered the greatness of dying." This discovery can only be attained if we identify the thought patterns that are keeping us from living life fully. The technique to achieve this: a kind of consciousness-altering rhythmic breathing done in time with music and sounds, all of which will help us find the cause of our blockages.

Symptoms that indicate the proximity of death and that we'll experience at the workshop: dry mouth, dry skin, garbled speech, the urge to return home and reconcile oneself with someone, weight loss, feebleness, fragile bones, vomiting, the desire to defecate and expel everything alien to us, death rattles, spasms, and glassy eyes.

The workshop is to death what a simulation is to an earthquake. Except, perhaps, for the minor detail that no one will escape death. Before going to bed we're tasked with drawing a self-portrait. I scribble a monstrosity à la Frida Kahlo with a spiny heart and a computer mouse chained to my wrist. Inside my stomach I draw a Gabriela with two heads: one is smiling and the other is crying. A drawing clearly meant to impress a psychologist, I think.

When I get into bed I start to feel the first effects of the workshop: I can't help remembering the awful bedsores on my grandmother Victoria's body. Unable to communicate and unable to recognize us, I find it hard to believe she was able to say goodbye or experience any beauty in her final moments. I think, too, about the last time I saw my grandmother Elena alive; she had been blind from diabetes for several years, and was on a trolley in the corridor of a public hospital waiting for a bed. She asked me for water, so I gave her a sip from a plastic cup. She said: "I'm going to die, love. Please take me home, I don't want to die here." I lied to her: "You're not going to die, Grandma." I kissed her on the forehead and left. She died an hour later in that same corridor.

I haven't been to the doctor for five years. Not even for a miserly check-up. Ever since I gave birth I've felt immortal, or at least I've forced myself to feel that way. I usually only let myself get sick with things a visit to the pharmacy can take care of, but lately I've been feeling strange. I don't know how to explain it, I just haven't been feeling well. One day, I finally decide to make an appointment with my doctor, who orders a blood test to see what's going on. It's ridiculous, but every time I leave a consulting room after having gotten good news, I'm slightly disappointed that I'm not really ill. So, when the nurse takes my blood pressure and tells me "It's really high," something inside me gloats, feeling vindicated. I don't truly want to be sick, of course, but my ego can't seem to handle being insignificant in any context, even in a hospital. It's an impulsive, unhealthy delight, revenge for all these years of perfect health. "150/109," says the nurse. "It should be closer to 139/89."

I'm thirty-five years old. I'm a woman. In other words, I'm young and drowning in progesterone. These two factors are arguably better than a life insurance policy worth a million euros. 2-0, death. I win. But it turns out I don't. For the whole of the next week I stuff myself with vegetables and don't eat salt, but when I go back my pressure is at 158/110. The nurse takes my blood pressure in my right arm and my left, three times each. Finally, my condition merits the presence of his scientific eminence, the doctor himself, who comes out and starts whispering with the nurses.

While I wait, my blood pressure goes through the roof—159/115. The doctor says this is not a one-off increase. Nor is it stress, even if I sometimes feel as if I'm going to explode in the middle of everything, like a bomb planted by a terrorist who's got the wrong target.

My father found out he had high blood pressure at thirty-five, my current age, and he's taken medication every day since. My grandfather died of a heart attack aged sixty; my grandmother Victoria from a brain hemorrhage. The game's turned against me. 3-2. I'm hypertensive. I suffer from stage 1 arterial hypertension. That's all. "But is there any chance the high blood pressure could be a symptom of something worse? How much worse?" Something horrible, probably, because the doctor looks at the tip of his shoe. "The test will tell us," he concludes.

Chronic arterial hypertension is the principal cause of death in the world, ahead of even hunger and cancer and AIDS. "The silent plague of the West," as it's called, restricts blood flow, increasing the chances of suffering from cardiovascular and renal diseases. The cause is unknown in 90 percent of cases, but almost always has to do with genetics and poor habits. Cue my ancestors' deficient arteries and my general unhealthiness.

I'm not fat, but that's definitely not by virtue of any effort of mine. And this is a condition I've always been proud of; it makes me feel alive and lively. I drink, I smoke, I go out, I get drunk once a week and once a week I die of a hangover, sometimes I take drugs, I eat junk food, I hate most vegetables, I'm a mother, I'm not baptized, I work in an office, I'm someone's wife, I stream TV series until three in the morning, I don't exercise, I spend ten hours a day in front of a screen and the only part of my body that gets any exercise are my fingers hitting the keyboard. It's a miracle my ass isn't the size of Brazil. Oh, and I love salt. Coarse-grain salt especially, those tiny diamonds on a good piece of steak, or in dips and sauces so salty they make me salivate with excitement. When I was a girl, my rotten DNA compelled me to sneak surreptitiously into the kitchen when my grandmother stepped away from the stove and sink my index finger into the red salt jar and run away. For a long time, sucking my salty finger while I watched my favorite cartoons was a version of happiness.

Things were once beautiful. Seriously, they were. Hangovers were manageable. And devouring hamburgers and fried chicken had no long-term consequences whatsoever. I can't say exactly when this impunity ended, but it was probably around the time I turned thirty. I didn't take the hint and carried on living in the only way I knew how, that is, believing I was immortal, never reading the labels on products, and publicly declaring myself an enemy of the fitness empire. Only every now and again a glitch in the matrix made me think that something might not be right, a slight acceleration in my pulse rate, for example, as if an unruly drummer had snuck into the magnificent chamber orchestra of my chest.

I run a hand over my stomach and verify it's still the round, four-month pregnancy bump I've grown accustomed to. I stroke my neck and feel my growing double chin. I stopped worrying about my reflection in shop windows some time ago. Now, I prefer to look away and imagine a different body for myself.

Back at home, I have to follow a strict diet that will turn me into the kind of person I wouldn't bother talking to even if we were stuck in an elevator together. I'm not allowed to drink alcohol, at most a glass of wine or two. I can't conceive of going to a bar without getting drunk, so I stop going out. My girlfriends promise they'll give up lines and gin and tonics for me, that they'll switch to spliffs and white wine, but I can tell they're lying. I start to consider finding new friends. I have to give up salt, and feel like I might as well give up eating altogether.

The scenario wouldn't be complete without a dose of pharmaceuticals. Every day, for three months to start with, I have to take two five-milligram tablets of Enalapril. The box of sixty costs a disconcerting twenty cents, and the list of possible side effects takes up half the leaflet. Am I supposed to fill my body with these cheap pills for the rest of my life? One day I meet a friend who tells me he has the same condition, that he spends his days eating garlic and doesn't take blood pressure tablets because "they kill your sex drive."

I suffer various episodes of anxiety thinking I could have a heart attack at any moment, and, as if that wasn't enough, I'm getting my blood pressure measured so often that I've become really popular in the local pharmacies. One night, like every night, I take off my clothes in front of the mirror and see a slight red mark on my right breast, just beside my nipple. I touch it. It's a hard lump. It wasn't there before, I'm sure of that. Then I scream.

LIVE YOUR DEATH DIARY, PART ONE

The first part of this essay was written with the ironic distance I almost always assume because I believe I write better from afar. Except I want this to be personal, otherwise it wouldn't be fair to the workshop leaders or the people here opening themselves up to others wholeheartedly. Nor would it be fair to readers or to myself. What follows is an extract from the journal I wrote over that weekend:

They've taken our phones away, so I don't know what time it is. I'm dead tired. We have to go back in an hour. Today we're doing breathing exercises. The morning was fun. We danced for two hours—electronica, salsa, and a ridiculous song called "My Tantric Boyfriend." Then we did contact exercises with partners: looking each other in the eye without talking, touching each other, hitting each other. I was with a really hot, muscly guy; his caresses made me tremble. I liked the exercise where you had to talk nonstop while the other person listened without saying a word. I talked about my family, about Jaime and Lena. My partner, a young girl this time, was really sad. She said it made her happy to know I was happy. It made me feel good about my life. She cried and I couldn't say anything to her because I wasn't allowed to. This is part of the double experience: repressing the desire to help the other person because in reality, when the moment comes, no one can help you. We all die alone.

What I liked most about the morning was the guiding exercise. I was a terrible guide and almost killed my blindfolded partner, an older man. I made him run and bump into things so often that he couldn't finish the exercise. When it was my turn to be blind, my partner was incredibly loving. He took me outside, made me smell and touch the grass, splash myself with water from the fountain, feel the breeze and the warmth of the sun. The workshop seems to be softening us all. Every time we do an exercise, somebody cries.

After we ate, I saw a boy who lives here playing with two dogs. I remembered that the director told us to want something badly. That's what I want, I thought, for Lena to have a huge, sunny garden and dogs to play with. I want to bring her up to be happy.

Are my eyes shining like everyone else's? Is a pious smile permanently plastered on my face? No—what I'm trying to get out of this workshop repels the glow taking over the rest of the group. On the one hand, I feel as though I've got to be somewhat critical if I'm to get a story out of this. After all, death is a show that is broadcast live and direct, and emulating it isn't going to alleviate our fear of the void. On the other hand, my affected cynicism might be keeping me from fully committing to anything, let alone this weekend. This workshop is full of dysfunctional, lonely, sad people who feel pain and don't know where it comes from. Am I superior to them because I don't take myself seriously, or does my stream of witticisms make me the exact opposite?

LIVE YOUR DEATH DIARY, PART TWO

The session finished at nearly two in the morning. Today half of us emulated death and tomorrow the other half will have a go. It's my turn tomorrow, so today I was in charge of bearing witness to the death of a group member. Caregivers were asked not to intervene in the other person's experience even if they seem to be suffering. We can only act if they ask us to. My dying person was a woman in her forties. I spent long hours by her side wetting her lips and holding a plastic bag so that she could vomit.

We sat in a circle, like in a ritual. In fact, the workshop is inspired by shamanic ayahuasca sessions. When we were all in position, the music started. The workshop leader guided the session, playing drums and encouraging the dying members by asking them to be brave and let go. The music is key because it makes you travel through different emotional states, from the most violent to the most peaceful. In a way, the workshop leader was a kind of DJ. He played everything from insufferable mystical songs to Wagner's *Ride of the Valkyries*. The breathing exercise was similar to patterned labor breathing: short, rhythmic inhalations and exhalations. When someone complained about the pain, you could ask the workshop leader to come over and move them. He would press down on some muscle until the person felt a sharp pain and cried out with relief.

I saw people laughing and crying, writhing in pain, shouting as if something had shattered into a thousand pieces inside them. When my dying woman seemed to be at peace, I covered her with a sheet. She was gone.

I've rarely been close to death. Perhaps that's why I'm so afraid of it. My parents always tell the story of when, as a very little girl, I first learned that people die. From that day on, whenever they mentioned someone to me, I would ask, "And have they died yet?"

Children see death as something strange and fascinating. I don't know at what point death stops being a word in a fairy story and becomes an inevitability. We spend a large part of our lives thinking of death as something remote and, above all, alien, until this delusion gives way to the realization that one day, we too will expire irredeemably—a painful realization for a vaguely intelligent pessimist with precarious religious beliefs. More so than death itself, which is already terrifying enough, humans fear the anonymity of disappearing. Philip Larkin puts it best: "*No rational being / Can fear a thing it will not feel*, not seeing / That this is what we fear—no sight, no sound, / No touch or taste or smell, nothing to think with, / Nothing to love or link with, / The anesthetic from which none come round."

The first person I knew who died was my grandfather Carlos. I was nine years old and my parents told me two days after the funeral. I didn't even see his coffin. I've never gone up to see the body in open-casket wakes. I didn't see the bodies of dead dogs. I barely dared to peek into the room at the funeral parlor where my mother was dressing my grandmother Elena. I saw her foot, dropping to one side in the same comfortable position it used to be in when she was listening to the radio in bed. It was like seeing her alive. I didn't see the body of my grandmother Victoria because when she finally died I was already in Spain. The only coffin I dared look into was my grandfather Maximo's, and only because I hardly knew him.

I've never seen the dead face of anyone I love. This ranks highly in my list of terrifying things.

I've been scared I'll die countless times, especially on airplanes, but only once did I truly think I was done for. A furious wave crashed onto me, and, struggling to surface in this whirlpool of foam, I thought I was going to die. During the civil war years in Peru, I was more afraid of death than ever. I expected a car bomb to blow up in my face or for someone to come after my journalist father and kill the rest of his family for good measure. Ever since I had a daughter, I've been constantly afraid I'll die. I'm so afraid I don't walk under scaffolding on buildings and always wait for the light to change before crossing the street. As I wait at train stations, I look over my shoulder to make sure a psychopath won't push me onto the tracks. If a neo-Nazi insults me, I no longer say anything back.

Dinner at our friend's house; her father is dying of cancer: "It's hard to care for someone who's dying, they go from a bad mood to a terrible one in a matter of minutes," she says. A few days later a friend's mother dies. Another aggressive cancer. My father and his brother both overcame bowel cancer a few years ago. In other words, my genes aren't only riddled with hypertension, there's cancer and diabetes in there as well. I have the sneaking suspicion that a crow has landed on my tree. I haven't made a will, I don't have a dying wish, and I can't imagine how my life will be like if I'm not in it.

Sometimes I wonder if I'm not externalizing my frenzied consumption of five seasons of *Six Feet Under*. I haven't watched anything else in the last two months and I feel alienated, as if I were on the verge of death. Someone dies at the beginning of every episode; in other words, over the course of five seasons the show introduces us to sixty fresh new ways to die: diseases, murders, freak accidents, peacefully, prematurely, violently. An episode in the show gets me thinking about the date on which I'll die. If I live out my whole life and die naturally at an average age, I could die in the year 2050. My grandfather is ninety-three years old and in perfect health, so if I've been lucky enough to inherit his genes I might make it to 2060. But I definitely won't see 2070. According to the website thedayofyourdeath.com, I'll die aged sixty-two. "You have 9,907 days, 00 hours, 14 minutes, and 56 seconds left," it warns me. Yourfears.com says I'll commit suicide on December 30, 2040 after losing everything. Mydeath. com thinks I'll die in 2024 in a paragliding accident. According to beingdead.com, my husband will beat me to death two years from now. There are lots of videos on the internet of people talking to themselves and saying how they think they'll die. They're fun. I watch a twenty-year-old girl say she's going to die of breast cancer aged thirty, and that she's known this since she was a girl, although she's completely healthy for now.

In *Swimming in a Sea of Death*, David Rieff writes about the illness and death of his mother, Susan Sontag, and about her deep fear of death. He quotes a phrase from her diary: "Death is unbearable unless you can get beyond the I." Rieff assures us that, unlike other people, Sontag wasn't able to overcome the "I." Unlike Bertolt Brecht, whose final poems, says Rieff, discuss the artist's reconciliation with the fact of death. Brecht sees a bird sitting in a tree, whose beautiful song he thinks is made lovelier by the knowledge that when he dies the bird will continue to sing. "Now I managed to enjoy the song of every blackbird after me too," he wrote. Sontag, meanwhile, wounded by mortality, left us this phrase: "In the valley of sorrow, spread your wings."

My scream startles my husband. Jaime runs to the bedroom and finds me crying and clutching at my breast.

"It's massive! Why didn't you notice it before? It's red, can you see?"

"Yes, it's red."

First thing tomorrow we'll go to the hospital. I look at myself in the mirror again and again. I'm scared to touch it. It wasn't there a few days ago; I would have noticed it. Jaime tells me that if it is a tumor, and we're not sure that it is, it'll be treatable. I remember the scene in Rieff's book when he describes how they removed Sontag's breast, an incredibly violent operation that, to get rid of all the diseased cells, had to gouge out a large part of her chest muscle.

I close my eyes. I'm tired. It's exhausting being an adult, having to take care of everything. I've often wanted to get ill so people will look after me and I won't have to do anything. I'd be so happy if I could stay in bed watching TV series all the time and sucking liquid food through a straw! I've repeated this dangerous mantra so many times that I ask myself if this unmentionable desire has anything to do with the lump in my breast.

That night, Jaime and I won't play our morbid little game. We won't talk about who'll die first, in which ocean we'll scatter the other's ashes, and who we'd choose to remarry. It's not funny anymore. We say nothing and wait for dawn.

The oncology ward shares a hallway with the maternity ward. From the waiting room, I watch the husbands pace and the doctors who bring life into the world. At last it's my turn. The nurse asks me to go in alone. I hear a baby cry.

The doctor examines me. She feels my breasts: "I can see it," she says, "I can feel it." I nearly faint.

While she touches my boob I try to cling to something else. All I can think of is the book I'm reading at the time, *Other Lives but Mine* by Emmanuel Carrère, a story of the death of a child and the death of a mother. In it, I'd found a reference to the spectacular book *Mars* by Fritz Zorn, a bestseller that the Swiss writer delivered in extremis to his publishers days before dying. In the book, he sticks a finger in the wound of the relationship between an insipid life and cancer. From the book's opening: "I'm young and rich and educated, and I'm unhappy, neurotic, and alone. I come from one of the best families on the east shore of Lake Zurich, the shore that people call the Gold Coast. My upbringing has been middle class, and I have been a model of good behavior all my life . . . And of course I have cancer. That follows logically enough from what I have just said about myself . . . [Cancer] is a psychic disorder and I can only regard its onset in an acute physical form as a great stroke of luck."

Jaime is waiting for me outside. I go out and smile at him. He smiles back. I sit on his knee. I hug him. He hugs me back.

I've only got non-puerperal mastitis, an inflammatory lesion of the breast.

My eyes are covered and my caregiver promises she'll be watching over me. I breathe deeply, I breathe and I breathe and I breathe, but all I can think about is being there, in this room, watched by these people. I'm thinking, unbelievably, that all these people failed to see how nice of a person I really am. I'm light-years away from reconciliation and equanimity. Or maybe these are my survival instincts kicking in to prevent me from going over to the other side. But I carry on, I try, I breathe increasingly rhythmically. This is hard, maybe I should've just taken LSD and saved myself all this work. The *Star Wars* theme playing in the background helps me concentrate. It's ridiculous, I know, but it reminds me of Jaime and Lena. I picture them. I hear some of the others shouting, having started their journeys. I feel almost cathartic now. My back starts hurting and I ask the workshop leader for help. He comes and twists my shoulder blade. The pain is intense. He says in my ear: "Shout, Gabriela, shout, what would you say to your mother?" I don't know where he got that about my mother, maybe from my drawing or my psychological evaluations. The only thing I know is that it works. I cry like a little girl, like I did on nights that were too dark: "Mom, Mmm, Mooom!" I cry like I haven't for years. I cry so much I ask myself if I'll ever be able to stop crying. I cry and remember that I'm not the little girl any more, that there's another little girl now and that I have to look after her. I cry because I'm everyone's daughter: my mother's, my husband's, my daughter's. I cry because I'm scared I'll fail as a mother. I say sorry to my little one for being the infantile person

I am. I promise I'll be solid, patient, and happy for her. Then I give myself over to the most absolute darkness, I allow it to come, to wrap me as if I'm being embraced by an enormous animal that swallows me and spits out my bones. I become a part of its shining pelt. The darkness is warm for the first time, like a black sun; my mind expands inside it. I'm empty now, but I'm not sad because I haven't lost anything. I'm taking with me everything I am. And now I see the beautiful landscape and the blessed light at the end of the tunnel—the cultural fantasy of resurrection and the intuition of mystery—the path to the suspension of all pain, of all fear. I smile to myself. If this is what death is like I don't mind dying tomorrow. I feel someone covering me with a sheet. I'm gone.

The good news is that you do come round from this anesthesia. The following day, in the final meeting where we describe our experiences, the workshop leader suggests that I make a list of the things that do me good and another of the things that do me harm.

Things that do me harm: being connected to the internet all day, checking Facebook, KFC, alcohol, drugs, not being with my daughter, my infantilism, the literary world, the pressure of having to write, people's contempt, frivolity, injustice, not being in Lima, salt, not exercising, judging others, judging myself.

Things that do me good: sex, Lena's love, Jaime's love, giving love, being loved, cooking, writing, sleeping, going out and seeing the sun, watching TV series with Jaime, laughing, doing absolutely nothing, tenderness, not being in Lima, crying, eating healthily without salt.

It's time to leave the workshop and apply its teachings in daily life. The participants have suddenly become best friends. They exchange emails, make plans, and tell each other about new workshops where they can meet again.

It hasn't been one of the most important experiences of my life, as that girl had promised, but I do feel good—so much so that I go for a walk alone in the countryside. Feeling fulfilled, I follow a path that goes into the woods. I walk and walk without looking back, and, all of a sudden, I stop still, look around me, and become myself again: I worry an animal will come out and eat me and I want to go home, to the only place where I feel safe.

I'm getting rid of Lena's nits while she watches TV with her friend Gael. She caught nits at school again. I drag one out with the comb and kill it. Lena is watching a show where a cartoon fish dies. A friend explains to her that after death, there are three possible paths: you either disappear, go to heaven, or reincarnate.

"What would you come back as?" I ask Lena, but she doesn't answer.

"What would you come back as, Gael? I'd come back as a tree, for example . . . "

"I'd be a lion."

"And what about you, Lena?" I press her. "A flower? A butterfly?"

"As me, end of . . . "

The blood tests showed no problem with cholesterol, kidney function, or blood sugar. I'm absolutely fine except for my blood pressure. My diet is pretty boring and I've managed to lose plenty of weight. They'll check my blood pressure again in three months, and if it carries on like it is now, they'll probably increase my dose of Enalapril and I'll keep taking it for life. Beyond that, everything is unpredictable.

I don't know yet where I want my ashes to be scattered. A good place would be in the Nanay River, which goes past Manacamiri, a small village near Iquitos in the Peruvian Amazon, where Jaime and I were really happy once. Or perhaps, so as to not suffer from exoticism, in the Mar de Grau, in Lima, where I hope to return one day. Or maybe, in the time I've got left, I'll find another place to spread my wings in this valley of sadness and joy.

On my imaginary headstone, death is still a blank space to be filled. And rain makes the weeds grow.

IMPOSSIBLE INTERVIEW
WITH MY ABUSER

TACKED TO THE WALL, my drawings and I peered at each other. It felt like there were fifty monsters hiding behind the closed doors of my wardrobe. I remember the drops of blood splattered across the blue of the room. Blue and red. I remember those colors in the soft light filtering through the amber glass of my window. And that day was breaking.

It had been a rough night. I had watched as he smashed his fist through the parchment paper lampshade that he had created himself, each pane printed with a photograph taken by him. One was a portrait of me with my eyes closed. Relationships are sometimes built on symbols, and in this one I was a genie trapped in a lamp. Every night when I went to bed, I read by the lamp's dim light poems by Oliverio Girondo, like this one:

> *the lovers who glance at each other,*
> *intuit each other,*
> *desire, caress, kiss,*
> *bare and pierce each other,*
> *embed, bombard, clinch,*
> *graft and twine each other,*
> *revive, collapse, beam,*
> *pry and tooth each other,*

inflame, disperse, bind,
maul and murder each other.

When its light was on, the lamp projected my face onto the wall like a shadow puppet, weightless. I used to call it the "peace lamp," because it was a gift given to win me back after one of our break-ups. It seemed important to keep it on, but that night he smashed it to bits because he had caught me kissing a close female friend.

It hurt to see him destroy his own work, his love.

I still have some tatters of my paper face in a drawer some-where. In that moment, though, the day was still ahead of us.

My first thought was whether I would be able to get the bloodstains off the wall. If my mother found them, she would be furious, especially at him, and it would be hard for us to see each other again. That was the first thing I thought. I felt the pain only afterward, when I looked in the mirror and screamed. I watched him kneel down, wrap his arms around my legs and cry and say "no, no, no," while my fractured nose wouldn't stop bleeding. I think I would have forgiven him then and there—sometimes I think I did forgive him then and there—if time had stopped in that moment. Maybe we would have been able to exist in that balance between aggression and guilt, pain and forgiveness. But time went on; it had to. Something leapt out of the lamp that night, and unlike paper and faces, shadows can't break.

I agreed to do this because I knew you would ask about that "punch," he said. I was going to use that as the title to this piece—an interview I did with him a few months ago. I chose it because of his quote marks, which seemed to me a sign that we had traversed radically different paths in our understanding of that act. To him, the blow that required surgery has a figurative meaning other than the reality of his closed fist breaking a bone in my face. Instead of finding another word, he chooses to circumscribe this one with quotation marks around it, perhaps to quote me, and by doing so create distance, irony.

In his version, I spoke to him of another man I went out with after we broke up. He says that I told him about a particular scene that upset him—some amorous or sexual experience. That it must have been the way I said it. That it was something that incensed him.

I concede that we were both good at throwing stones at each other. He would throw one and I would throw it right back. But in that exchange it wasn't really him I wanted to do away with. Rather, it was everything he represented, all the things that still lacked a name in my head. I was fighting against something bigger using only my intuition, because I still lacked the language, the maturity, and the tools to understand the world and what it had done to us. So did he. But over time, the struggle has taken on another form. I have learned to recognize myself and recognize the narratives I want to transform, that I *need* to transform in order to survive. And I think something inside me expected something similar of him—expected that the process set off by breaking a loved one's nose and the pain initiated after a loved one fractures you would eventually converge.

We first met at a birthday party. We felt happily out of place because we were the oldest ones there, and that gave us a license for transgression. I invited him into the bathroom with me. I played the part well: captivating, troubled, assertive. He was amused and went along. Some kids were playing around and opened the bathroom door as a prank, catching us mid-obscenity. The rumor of what had just happened spread through the house and we became personae non grata. We decided to go. I hopped onto his bike and, zigzagging back to his house, we felt like runaways of the world. That's what we identified as. According to him, everything that happened between us from then on was "a gradual betrayal of that night."

It's a good phrase. It is also a lie. He used it countless times during the course of our relationship, but only when he felt that I had wronged him. As a result, the phrase that could have been used to express our mutual and ineluctable responsibility in the fall of an idealized romance, was turned, each time he used it, into a new accusation.

It wasn't the first or the last time that a man who professed to love my freedom and to find my crimes captivating began to behave as though he hated all of the above. Inevitably, in their eyes, I would go from being a girl on fire to being the fire itself—voracious in my destructiveness.

The world is full of boring lepidopterist types who like to attract ungovernable women and then pin them to a board for their butterfly collection. Men who like to fall in love with the slut and bring her home so that she can continue to be slutty—but for him only. Or who try to make her pure again. All my male romantic partners have wanted me to say that they were the first stranger I'd sucked off in the bathroom, and they always wanted to be the last. They expected me to be grateful for getting me off the streets and showing me the hidden wonders of the world. When they eventually found out none of this was the case, that I had a history that I intended to keep writing, trouble began.

How to evolve when a woman wants to write her own story, and a man wants her to be a blank, immaculate notebook, ready for him to fill with words and images in his own unmistakable style?

Some people aren't interested in how we write; instead, they want to do the writing for us. Some, like him, are even capable of withstanding or submitting themselves to the pain "we cause them" (this time the quote marks are mine) just to have an excuse to access a perverse kind of masculinity.

When we love someone we allow them to tear out a few of our pages. Sometimes our notebook becomes quite thin and fragile. They rip out some of our darkest and most luminous pages, but we help, too. I admit I tore out many of my own pages because I thought that if I mutilated myself I would be more deserving of love.

I remember something he wrote to me in a letter when we separated for a period: "Thinking of you with another is poison in my blood."

I poisoned his blood.

"The idea, as always, is to talk about myself," I said to him.

"Hey, baby, when you write, you're the hero of your shit," he said, stealing from Bukowski. I was surprised that he agreed to do the interview, and for it to be published with his real name and his photograph. I said that, if it all went well, he would be my new idol. He poked fun at my hope that we'd both end up

217

happy with the result. "I don't think either of us will be happy. But since I can't correct your questions, I claim the same right with my answers," he said, and I reiterated my good faith.

My intention was to settle our mutual pending debts, to have a conversation where two people who desired, loved, and hurt each other when they were very young come together after many years and analyze their relationship in the light of everything they have since learned and processed. To me, that new light is feminism. Might it be the same to him? What other lens could exist through which to look at the kind of couple we were, at the act he is determined on enclosing in quotation marks?

Our relationship had ended very badly. We spent three turbulent years together, during the last of which the fighting had escalated. He physically abused me out of jealousy, we both slept with other people, I'd had an abortion, he had disappeared, I had started seeing someone else who I then left to get back together with him, we had given each other space, but we had not been able to completely stop seeing each other. When I finally told him it was over, it took us another few years to complete the slow uncoupling of our bodies.

At some point our process seemed to have reached closure at last. We'd talked a few times in recent years and we seemed capable of sitting down maturely to take a look at what happened.

I spent several intense days preparing for the interview. I wrote out a few questions about different aspects of our relationship, each one referencing an episode that marked us as a couple: Do you think the way we met determined our fate at all? Do you think we actively disliked each other at the time? Weren't we both too in love with ourselves? How many times do you think we repeated the cycle of misery? Do you interpret the punch as a manifestation of *machista* violence?

His answers took several days to arrive. To summarize: he wanted to prove that his violence toward me was equivalent to my violence against the world. He described me as "psychopathic," and as evidence, he used two stories: the story of one night when we had just met, when I got drunk and yelled horrible things at my sister and threw a plant pot out the window, nearly hitting a friend of his. I remember that day because I was really nervous about him coming to a party at my house for the first time. I was so anxious that I completely overhauled my room, replacing stuffed animals with books and plants to impress him. I was extremely insecure at the time. And, I admit, I put people around me in danger.

The other episode that he gloated over during the interview took place one morning when we were just back from a frustrated trip where I had lost a waist bag with all of his money in it. After crying for hours and begging forgiveness, I woke him up with a slap on the face. There is no justification for that, either, and I regret it deeply.

Even though my open hand hadn't left the faintest mark on his skin, he called it a punch to equate it to his closed fist breaking my nose, insisting that his was a blow that had followed a similar blow. When editing the interview, I proposed changing the word "punch" for "slap." I also asked him to remove the mention of me insulting my sister and calling her "bitch," so as to not involve her in all of this. He accused me of trying to "soften the facts" and did not accept any of the changes I proposed.

Are women sometimes aggressors? Do we sometimes attack the people we love the most—our sisters, our partners? Of course. Though I have rarely physically attacked anyone, I come from a long line of explosive women. My mother and her mother are the perfect examples—they both go far beyond assertiveness during arguments. I know that many of my demands, the sometimes brutal ways in which I say things, my stinging and sometimes unnecessary honesty, my rampant lack of discretion, my appalling timing, my invasive attitude, my confused notions of respect and self-respect, my jealousy and fragility in the presence of anyone I find threatening, my low self-esteem, and my intermittent inability to put myself in others' shoes have all caused pain to the people I've shared my life with. Anyone conducting a basic evaluation might reach similar conclusions about themselves: we all have the potential to cause harm and pain. Even a child. And anyone should be able to apologize for this pain without hesitation, without trying to justify something as heinous as physical assault.

But it just so happens that sexist men have trouble admitting their mistakes. They can't seem to do it without beating around the bush and appealing to biology, psychology, anthropology, and sociology, which become potholes in the road toward account-ability and healing.

Yes, everyone can be violent, but by no means does that make all aggressions equal. The difference between gender violence and other forms of aggression is that in the former, being a woman is what puts us in a vulnerable and dangerous position. Gender violence blooms where men attempt to exercise control over women's social connections, professional development, and sexuality. This abuse is unequivocally the product of systematic inequality, but to him, that blow can only be understood in the context of our relationship. "The issue is complex," he says. There are nuances, and I should accept that he has taught me a lesson with his irrefutable answers, with which he has managed to put a stop to my "ignoble intention" to sacrifice him in order to justify my "feminist crusade." To him, I had committed, as he puts it, "the greatest crime from the beginning of civilization: betrayal."

I failed in my attempt to have a conversation about sexism and the structural violence we all experience, especially when we're young and know nothing about imposed monogamy, romantic love, the oppression of bodies and desires, and gender violence. I was not able to get him to examine his privilege as a heterosexual man of a specific class. I failed spectacularly, and didn't publish the interview.

I was afraid publishing the interview would allow him to rewrite his actions and would create a forum for those who like to say: "that's what you get for being a slut, for fooling around, for being violent, for being crazy," or, "you were just a pair of kids hurting each other," as if there were no underlying structural issues to address.

His name is not here, and neither is his photograph. And that's because I have stopped caring about him as an individual. He represents only my old enemy, the macho, in its first incarnation.

The year prior to the incident had been the hardest of my life. I had found out that my father had another partner and another daughter. I felt deceived, wounded, as if I were the betrayed wife. Before my twentieth birthday, I had already been through many hellish experiences—drugs, two abortions, and two rounds of psychotherapy. I was filled with pain when anyone rejected me, and this partner did so countless times, which led to perverse power dynamics. I was a young woman in search of the next extreme adventure. All I wanted was to dilute myself. Not to be me.

When I first met him, I wasn't able to look after myself, let alone anyone else. Now that my life consists of caring for others and bringing up kids and figuring out how to do a better job of it, I am finally able to see all my failings. And to admit that I was often a bad partner. I acted impulsively out of jealousy. Other times I was not honest and I behaved with guile. I played with things no one should play with. And I lost.

Jealousy is normal; what isn't normal is to hit someone out of jealousy. Because he was incapable of acknowledging how fragile and threatened other men made him feel, he charged against me. To this day, he is convinced that I wielded my sexuality in a way meant to make him suffer. He accused me of cruelly telling him that two guys had screwed me in a park and that I had hooked up with another guy at a nightclub in Cusco and we'd had sex "without exchanging a word" in the room I shared with my friends.

What did he say about his having "punched" me? He said that in the middle of an argument, I'd gone back to my "stories," this time telling him about the guy I had been with when we weren't together. He accused me of not knowing how to be alone. He told me that his "anger and frustration" had been translated into an "apocalyptic blow." He reminded me that he had asked for forgiveness immediately after. Those who hit hard, caress afterward. I know that well. He admitted it was one of the most shameful events in his life.

"If you consider it to be within the category of machista abuse, I will concede that. My memory is that of profound powerlessness and frustration, and then the deepest guilt." But then he went on to deliver his disquisition about human violence in general: "Abuse and violence are not exclusive to men, women also commit them in equal measure [sic], however, in this case, in this confrontation, nature left women at a disadvantage by giving them a lesser percentage of muscular mass. There are evolutionary reasons, basically to do with reproductive strategies, for this imbalance. I believe it's important to demystify the topic, I have seen much fanaticism around this, a kind of 'Taliban' feminism that does not allow for an honest and open conversation on the subject."

After reading his messages I felt weirdly guilty, confused, and undervalued. I, the strong, empowered, educated woman, journalist, and writer, a privileged person in so many ways, with an impossible interview in the wastebasket beside me, felt his words ringing in my head.

For years, I believed I was partly to blame for that blow. I believed it was merely the culmination of our own form of tainted love. I refused to think of myself as a victim. Now, I feel sad that I can still doubt whether the violence I experienced was gender violence. But it's even more upsetting that the person who brutally attacked me dares to relativize violence, justify it, to say it was a one-off, talk to me about the "context of the relationship," and in general seize the opportunity to do what he did during our entire relationship: to mansplain and to lecture constantly, always from a position of superiority and power, showing off his reasoning and argumentative capacity to emerge with the upper hand. Should it be up to him to put forward definitions of gender violence and stake out its limits? Is it up to him to decide what falls within the category, and what does not?

Giving full rein to my sexual freedom and telling stories about it has brought me many problems from a young age, especially with men. I have always been someone who desires and tells stories about what she desires. During my early twenties, I couldn't mention my sexual experiences without eliciting profound feelings of insecurity and violent reactions in the men around me. He was not the only one who felt that way, but he was the only one who hit me because of it.

Why was I not free to tell whatever stories I wanted without being punished? Even if I had been unfaithful and rubbed it in his face, even if I had some twisted desire to watch him suffer because of it, even if I was a goddamn sadist, which I am not, I should not have experienced that degree of violence.

But the freedom to say whatever we like is a small one compared to the freedom of being who we are. It was not only my voice that was lost every time I was silenced or decided to be silent. I now know that telling stories about my experiences is something inherent to me, a fundamental part of my identity, something that back then had already started to weave itself between creation and life. If that did not belong to me, then nothing else did.

Whatever kind of violence I may have committed against him is hardly comparable to the kind he exercised against me. His aggression is a criminal, classifiable offense. That is the difference. Even though we both harmed each other, even though the legal system in Peru is a joke, his was still a crime.

I accepted his apology and did not report it to the police at the time. But even if I had, the most that would have happened is that the medical examiner would have given me maybe ten days off work and he would have had to go to therapy for a few weeks. It's not just a matter of body mass.

Do thousands of women a year die because men are stronger, because they have more body mass, because biology was on their side in the distribution of physical vigor? Of course not. Do we die because we like to live dangerously, because we like to do and say provocative things that eat away at men's confidence until we drive them crazy and out of control? Of course not. Women die because they have dared to move a few fractions of an inch or several miles outside the sphere that patriarchy has relegated them to. Whether at home or in the workplace, on the streets or in intimacy, we die because there are men who are incapable of accepting us and themselves. We die because we like to (foolish as we are) act like we're equals.

And I am no longer talking about the kid who broke my nose in a fit of jealousy. I am talking about the grown man who seems to have not learned anything, the man who typed: "You exercised violence and you received it, Gabriela. Abuse and violence are not exclusive to men; women commit them in equal measure."

According to Peru's National Statistics Institute 2014 survey, thirty-two percent of Peruvian women experience physical violence from a spouse or partner at some point. The Peruvian national human rights office estimates that every month, ten women die at the hands of their partners. Another study reveals that from January 2009 to October 2015, 795 femicides were committed, but Peruvian courts issued only eighty-four sentences between 2012 and 2015. In 81 percent of the cases of attempted femicide, no measures were taken by authorities to protect survivors, and 24 percent of the women who sought government protection were later murdered by the men from whom they had sought protection. In 2017, between January and September, there were ninety-four femicides and 5,707 sexual assaults.

A woman's sexual freedom is not easy to comprehend for many men, especially in Peru. A feminist friend of mine explained: "If someone breaks your nose because of jealousy, that's gender violence. If someone breaks your nose because you exercise your sexual freedom and are empowered by it, that's gender violence. If someone beats you because you are vindicating your status as a free woman, that's gender violence. If someone breaks your nose because he believes you are his and no one else's, that's gender violence. If someone manipulates narratives to make you believe that it's abusive of you to tell stories about things he does not enjoy or that make him feel like an idiot, that's psychological and gender violence. If the abuse is physical and completely out of proportion with whatever might have instigated it, we are speaking of gender violence. If the proposed narrative is that our own violence lands us in hospitals, that's a machista narrative."

Twenty years on, the person who was my partner places the word "punch" in quotation marks. And I remove them. And when I do, the blow hurts less.

ABOUT THE AUTHOR

GABRIELA WIENER (Lima, 1975) is author of the *crónicas* collections *Sexografías*, *Nueve Lunas*, *Mozart, la iguana con priapismo y otras historias*, and *Llamada perdida*. Her work also includes the poetry collection *Ejercicios para el endurecimiento del espíritu*. Her latest book is *Dicen de mí* (2017). She writes regularly for the newspapers *El País* (Spain) and *La República* (Peru). She also writes for several American and European magazines, such as *Etiqueta Negra* (Peru), *Anfibia* (Argentina), *Corriere della Sera* (Italy), *XXI* (France), and *Virginia Quarterly Review* (United States). In Madrid, she worked as editor of the Spanish edition of *Marie Claire*. She left the magazine in 2014 to work on her first novel.

ABOUT THE TRANSLATORS

LUCY GREAVES is a literary translator and bike mechanic who lives in Bristol, UK. She enjoys the poetry of bicycles and the mechanics of language equally.

JENNIFER ADCOCK is a poet and translator working in English and Spanish. Under the pen name "Juana Adcock," she has published *Manca* (2014) and has taken part in numerous literary festivals and events internationally. Her translations have appeared in *Words Without Borders*, *Asymptote*, *Guardian*, and *LitHub*. In 2016 she was named one of the "Ten New Voices from Europe" by the organization Literature Across Frontiers.

RESTLESS BOOKS is an independent, nonprofit publisher devoted to championing essential voices from around the world, whose stories speak to us across linguistic and cultural borders. We seek extraordinary international literature that feeds our restlessness: our hunger for new perspectives, passion for other cultures and languages, and eagerness to explore beyond the confines of the familiar. Our books—fiction, narrative nonfiction, journalism, memoirs, travel writing, and young people's literature—offer readers an expanded understanding of a changing world.

Visit us at www.restlessbooks.org.